Date: 10/1/12

363.7387 GLO
Global warming /

INTRODUCING ISSUES WITH OPPOSING VIEWPOINTS®

Global Warming

Lauri S. Scherer, *Book Editor*

GREENHAVEN PRESS
A part of Gale, Cengage Learning

GALE
CENGAGE Learning·

Detroit • New York • San Francisco • New Haven, Conn • Waterville, Maine • London

Elizabeth Des Chenes, *Director, Publishing Solutions*

For more information, contact:
Greenhaven Press
27500 Drake Rd.
Farmington Hills, MI 48331-3535
Or you can visit our Internet site at gale.cengage.com

For product information and technology assistance, contact us at

Gale Customer Support, 1-800-877-4253
For permission to use material from this text or product, submit all requests online at www.cengage.com/permissions

Further permissions questions can be e-mailed to permissionrequest@cengage.com

Articles in Greenhaven Press anthologies are often edited for length to meet page requirements. In addition, original titles of these works are changed to clearly present the main thesis and to explicitly indicate the author's opinion. Every effort is made to ensure that Greenhaven Press accurately reflects the original intent of the authors. Every effort has been made to trace the owners of copyrighted material.

Cover image © ribeiroantonio/ShutterStock.com.

LIBRARY OF CONGRESS CATALOGING-IN-PUBLICATION DATA

Global warming / Lauri S. Scherer, book editor.
    p. cm. -- (Introducing issues with opposing viewpoints)
  Includes bibliographical references and index.
  ISBN 978-0-7377-5681-4 (hardback)
  1. Global warming. 2. Global temperature changes. 3. Carbon dioxide I. Friedman, Lauri S.
  QC981.8.G56G574417 2012
  363.738'74--dc23

                                                                          2011047670

Printed in the United States of America
 2 3 4 5 6 7 16 15 14 13 12

Contents

Chapter 3: How Can Global Warming Be Minimized?

Foreword

Indulging in a wide spectrum of ideas, beliefs, and perspectives is a critical cornerstone of democracy. After all, it is often debates over differences of opinion, such as whether to legalize abortion, how to treat prisoners, or when to enact the death penalty, that shape our society and drive it forward. Such diversity of thought is frequently regarded as the hallmark of a healthy and civilized culture. As the Reverend Clifford Schutjer of the First Congregational Church in Mansfield, Ohio, declared in a 2001 sermon, "Surrounding oneself with only like-minded people, restricting what we listen to or read only to what we find agreeable is irresponsible. Refusing to entertain doubts once we make up our minds is a subtle but deadly form of arrogance." With this advice in mind, Introducing Issues with Opposing Viewpoints books aim to open readers' minds to the critically divergent views that comprise our world's most important debates.

Introducing Issues with Opposing Viewpoints simplifies for students the enormous and often overwhelming mass of material now available via print and electronic media. Collected in every volume is an array of opinions that captures the essence of a particular controversy or topic. Introducing Issues with Opposing Viewpoints books embody the spirit of nineteenth-century journalist Charles A. Dana's axiom: "Fight for your opinions, but do not believe that they contain the whole truth, or the only truth." Absorbing such contrasting opinions teaches students to analyze the strength of an argument and compare it to its opposition. From this process readers can inform and strengthen their own opinions, or be exposed to new information that will change their minds. Introducing Issues with Opposing Viewpoints is a mosaic of different voices. The authors are statesmen, pundits, academics, journalists, corporations, and ordinary people who have felt compelled to share their experiences and ideas in a public forum. Their words have been collected from newspapers, journals, books, speeches, interviews, and the Internet, the fastest growing body of opinionated material in the world.

Introducing Issues with Opposing Viewpoints shares many of the well-known features of its critically acclaimed parent series, Opposing Viewpoints. The articles are presented in a pro/con format, allowing readers to absorb divergent perspectives side by side. Active reading questions preface each viewpoint, requiring the student to approach the material thoughtfully and carefully. Useful charts, graphs, and cartoons supplement each article. A thorough introduction provides readers with crucial background on an issue. An annotated bibliography points the reader toward articles, books, and websites that contain additional information on the topic. An appendix of organizations to contact contains a wide variety of charities, nonprofit organizations, political groups, and private enterprises that each hold a position on the issue at hand. Finally, a comprehensive index allows readers to locate content quickly and efficiently.

Introducing Issues with Opposing Viewpoints is also significantly different from Opposing Viewpoints. As the series title implies, its presentation will help introduce students to the concept of opposing viewpoints and learn to use this material to aid in critical writing and debate. The series' four-color, accessible format makes the books attractive and inviting to readers of all levels. In addition, each viewpoint has been carefully edited to maximize a reader's understanding of the content. Short but thorough viewpoints capture the essence of an argument. A substantial, thought-provoking essay question placed at the end of each viewpoint asks the student to further investigate the issues raised in the viewpoint, compare and contrast two authors' arguments, or consider how one might go about forming an opinion on the topic at hand. Each viewpoint contains sidebars that include at-a-glance information and handy statistics. A Facts About section located in the back of the book further supplies students with relevant facts and figures.

Following in the tradition of the Opposing Viewpoints series, Greenhaven Press continues to provide readers with invaluable exposure to the controversial issues that shape our world. As John Stuart Mill once wrote: "The only way in which a human being can make some approach to knowing the whole of a subject is by hearing what can be said about it by persons of every variety of opinion and studying all modes in which it can be looked at by every character of mind. No wise man ever acquired his wisdom in any mode but this." It is to this principle that Introducing Issues with Opposing Viewpoints books are dedicated.

Introduction

As global warming becomes an increasingly pressing topic, policy makers and scientists are exploring the potential of a fascinating and innovative approach to climate control: geoengineering. The idea behind geoengineering is to use manmade devices or artificial methods that will change the way Earth's natural systems work and thus keep temperatures from rising. "Once the domain of scientists' off-hours schemes scrawled on cocktail napkins," writes *USA Today*'s science reporter Dan Vergano, "geoengineering is getting a serious look."[1]

The Royal Society of London has described geoengineering as "deliberate, large-scale manipulation of the planetary environment,"[2] and that is exactly what these imaginative solutions propose to do. One such proposal, called "ocean fertilization," suggests saturating the ocean with iron deposits, which would in turn encourage phytoplankton, a microscopic plant-like organism, to bloom. Like their much larger, land-based counterparts, these plankton absorb carbon dioxide and could in theory pull large amounts of that global warming–related gas from the air.

Another geoengineering idea is called "cloud engineering." The idea here is to mimic what clouds do naturally—reflect sunlight and keep Earth's temperature in check. Cloud engineering would involve genetically engineering crops to have shinier, more reflective surfaces, and features ideas to put enormous, floating, white blocks of Styrofoam in the ocean, which might also reflect light and keep ocean temperatures from rising. Engineers have also suggested creating more clouds via a method called "cloud seeding," which would involve creating clouds by spraying saltwater from the ocean into the sky.

Another fascinating idea is to saturate the atmosphere with sulfur aerosols, which are white particles that can reflect light. This idea was inspired by a natural cooling event: the 1991 eruption of Mount Pinatubo in the Philippines. This volcanic eruption spewed more than 15 million tons of sulfur dioxide into the atmosphere. The particles shot twenty-one miles up into Earth's stratosphere and circulated around the globe. According to the National Aeronautics and Space Administration's NASA Goddard Institute for Space Studies, the haze created by these particles scattered the sun's rays so much that it led to a worldwide cool of between 0.7 and 0.9 degrees in 1992 and 1993. Scientists have gotten ideas from the Mount Pinatubo eruption, and they have proposed to artificially send similar particles into the atmosphere to initiate another mass cooling. They have suggested getting the sulfur particles into the atmosphere by dropping them from balloons or planes, or even using cannons to fire them into the sky.

Forestation is another geoengineering idea getting attention from scientists. Planting trees to absorb carbon from the atmosphere is not a new idea and is already practiced many places in the world. But scientists have proposed planting genetically engineered trees that would require less water and feature specially designed trunks that could pull especially large amounts of carbon from the surrounding air. Some, such as Columbia University's Klaus Lackner, have even suggested planting artificial trees, machines covered with panels designed to suck carbon out of the environment. This idea, like the one to install hundreds of thousands of mirrors in space to reflect sunlight away from the Earth, is but one of the several geoengineering solutions proposed to curb global warming.

That these and other creative, cutting-edge proposals have captured humans' imagination is without question; whether they can effectively prevent global warming is of much greater debate. Many of the scientists who support geoengineering say such techniques could be the last, best hope to avert catastrophic climate change. Boston University professor Jay Michaelson points out that mainstream global warming solutions, such as investing in alternative energy sources, do not actually propose to reduce carbon-dioxide levels; rather, they merely propose to reduce the rate of how much new carbon dioxide enters the atmosphere each year. To actually get those levels reversing, he thinks something on a much grander scale will have to be attempted. "Either we have to question the nature of industrial society," he says, "or we have to consider other solutions."[3]

Yet opposition to, or at the very least, wariness of, many geoengineering ideas stems from the fact that they are untested and could have unforeseen consequences on other aspects of the environment. All the iron required for ocean fertilization, for example, could kill fish and add other greenhouse gases to the environment. Likewise, the suggestion to launch mirrors into space could end up littering Earth's upper atmosphere with an enormous amount of debris. Plus, this plan would likely come at tremendous cost: Rockets would need to be built to get the mirrors into space, and the fuel for such an endeavor would not only be expensive but threatening to the environment. *USA Today* reports that the fuel for the rockets would likely pump so much black soot into the environment that it would *increase* the average global temperature by more than a degree, which would defeat the purpose of sending the mirrors into space at all.

Beyond the individual failures, some scientists have an even greater worry: that some of these planetary alterations would not be able to be shut down once put in motion, putting humanity at even greater risk. "The history of intervening in complex systems to correct them is not good," says Ken Caldeira, an ecologist at Stanford University who has tentatively endorsed geoengineering strategies. "You always think you know how the system's going to respond, but we should assume that if we start doing this, there are going to be some ugly surprises."[4] Meteorologist Alan Robock agrees. "Scientists cannot possibly account for all of the complex climate interactions or predict all of the impacts of geoengineering," he warns. "With so much at stake, there is reason to worry about what we don't know."[5]

In fact, it is all the things that could go wrong with geoengineering that make it more dangerous than any projected effect from global warming, says science historian James Fleming. "Geoengineering is planetary-scale intervention [in]—or tinkering with—planetary processes. Period," he says. "I think it may be infinitely more dangerous than climate change, largely due to the suspicion and social disruption it would trigger by changing humanity's relationship to nature." Fleming counsels humanity to make decisions based not on what they can do in the future, but what they failed to do in the past—and to avoid, at all cost, being so arrogant to believe they can "fix the sky."[6]

It remains to be seen whether geoengineering can help avert catastrophic climate change or whether it will herald even more disastrous results. Geoengineering is among the many topics explored in *Introducing Issues with Opposing Viewpoints: Global Warming*. Students will also consider opposing arguments on whether global warming is occurring; whether humans are causing it; whether it poses a threat to civilization; and how its effects can be minimized. Guided reading questions and essay prompts will help students articulate their own opinions on this critical topic.

Notes

1. Dan Vergano, "Can Geoengineering Put the Freeze on Global Warming?" *USA Today*, February 25, 2011. www.usatoday.com/tech /science/environment/2011-02-25-geoengineering25_CV_N.htm.
2. Royal Society of London, "Geoengineering the Climate: Science, Governance and Uncertainty," September 1, 2009. http://royal society.org/Geoengineering-the-climate.
3. Quoted in Elizabeth Svodoba, "The Sun Blotted Out from the Sky," Salon.com, April 2, 2008. www.salon.com/news/feature /2008/04/02/geoengineering.
4. Quoted in Svodoba, "The Sun Blotted Out from the Sky."
5. Alan Robock, "20 Reasons Why Geoengineering May Be a Bad Idea," *Bulletin of the Atomic Scientists*, vol. 64, no. 2, May/June 2008, p. 17. www.thebulletin.org/files/064002006_0.pdf.
6. Quoted in David Biello, "Can Geoengineering Save the World from Global Warming?" *Scientific American*, February 25, 2011. www.scientificamerican.com/article.cfm?id=geoengineering-to -save-the-world-from-global-warming&print=true.

Chapter 1

Is Global Warming Occurring?

A three-dimensional graphic model provided by NASA's Ice, Cloud, and land Elevation Satellite (ICESat) is helping scientists understand how life on Earth is affected by a changing climate.

The Planet
Is Warming

Bryan Appleyard

"The disaster is coming much sooner than we thought."

In the following viewpoint Bryan Appleyard argues that the planet is warming. He takes readers through a history of climate change, arguing that key events during the Industrial Revolution kicked off a warming trend that continues to worsen today. He says people who deny the existence of global warming look at small samples of evidence or take evidence out of context. He says indications of global warming include melting ice, increased temperatures, worsening weather, and other clearly observable factors. He urges people to take the threat from global warming seriously and to listen to the scientists and climatologists who warn of its destructive potential.

Appleyard is a writer whose works have been published in various newspapers including the British paper *Sunday Times*, from which this viewpoint was taken.

AS YOU READ, CONSIDER THE FOLLOWING QUESTIONS:

1. What critical events related to global warming does Appleyard say took place during the Industrial Revolution?
2. What are current atmospheric carbon levels, according to Appleyard?
3. By what percent was summer sea ice diminished in 2007, according to the author?

There are so many good reasons not to believe in global warming: summers lately have been cool and wet; since 1998 global temperatures have actually fallen; dissident scientists say it's not happening; green believers are irritating—they wear Tibetan hats that only look good on Tibetans, and are so often wrong that they're probably wrong about the Big One; large parts of the punditocracy say it's all nonsense, usually that it's a left-wing plot against capitalism; the rainforest is growing back faster than it's being cut down and polar bears are, apparently, doing quite well. Global warming? Yeah, right! . . .

But if you suspend your prejudices and your vanity for a moment, everything changes. You find out that the following statements are true beyond argument.

The climate is warming. It is almost certain this is caused by emissions of greenhouse gases caused by human activity. Nobody has come up with an alternative explanation that stands up. If the present warming trend continues, nasty things will probably start happening to humans within the next century, possibly the next decade [beyond 2009]. Something must be done. If nothing is done, then the benign climatic conditions that have sustained human civilisation for 10,000 years are in danger of collapse to be replaced by . . . well, write your own disaster movie. . . .

A Shock to Planet Earth

Beginning from the beginning. In 1750 there were 800m [million] people in the world. Then came the Industrial Revolution. This required almost pure carbon, coal, oil and gas to be taken from the ground where it had lain for millions of years, burnt and tossed into the atmosphere as carbon dioxide. Now there are almost 7 billion of us and we toss 27 billion tons of carbon dioxide—7.3 billion tons of pure carbon—into the atmosphere every year. Since the Industrial Revolution, the total amount tossed is half a trillion tons of pure carbon. It is impossible to say this didn't happen and bone-headed madness to think it will have no effect. We are more or less certain that the effect has been a one-degree-centigrade rise in global temperature.

What do the deniers say about this? "The world's temperature rose about half a degree centigrade during the last quarter of the 20th century," writes Nigel Lawson, "but even the Hadley Centre for Climate

Since the beginning of the Industrial Revolution in the nineteenth century, approximately a half trillion tons of pure carbon have been released into the atmosphere.

Prediction and Research . . . has now conceded that recorded temperature figures for the first seven years of the 21st century reveal there has been a standstill."

Actually, er, bollocks. In the staff cafe at University College London, Chris Rapley draws me a graph showing temperature fluctuations over the past million years. He draws an even rising-and-falling line. Then he corrects himself and the even line becomes a jagged landscape of peaks and troughs. But the trend line remains clear. So yes, if you start in 1998—a very hot year thanks to an intense El Niño event in the South Pacific—and draw a line to a cool year, 2007, you get a falling line. Nevertheless, the average temperature for this decade is higher than the previous one. The trend is intact. Anyway, back to basics. Half a trillion tons of carbon came as a shock to planet Earth. Antarctic ice cores reveal that for about 1m years, atmospheric carbon fluctuated between ice-age levels of 180 parts per million (ppm) and warm levels of 280ppm. We don't know why this narrow fluctuation was so stable. It just was.

Rising Levels Amid Misguided Theories

Carbon levels are now at 387ppm and rising rapidly. The best we can hope for, if radical low-emission targets are accepted by world governments *now*, is to stabilise the figure at 450ppm. That will mean a further one-degree temperature rise. This could be nasty—more hurricanes, rising sea levels, spreading deserts, loss of arable land—but maybe manageably so.

At this point, deniers often talk about the medieval warm period. From about 800 A.D. to 1300 A.D., temperatures rose by, at one point, more than they are rising now. Fair enough, except this wasn't a global phenomenon, it was purely European. The Earth as a whole cooled.

Having lost that one, the next denialist move is the Sunspot Gambit, much in evidence in that Channel 4 documentary. Mention that show to Rapley and he loses his amiable manner. "I was scandalised. I shall never, ever, forgive Channel 4 and if I ever find a way of preventing them having public funds then I shall exercise it."

The idea behind the Sunspot Gambit is that global temperature trends are dependent on solar activity. Well, it's true, they are, a bit. But the idea that large-scale trends are caused by "solar forcing" is wrong. The good thing about being a Spottist is you can be right for 11 years at a time. That's the length of the sunspot cycle, so you can construct a theory based on one cycle and be sure that it will not be knocked down by the next for 11 years.

> **FAST FACT**
>
> According to a January 2011 report from the NASA Goddard Institute for Space Studies, global average surface temperatures in 2010 (the most recent year for which data are available) tied 2005 as the warmest temperature since records began in 1880. The temperature trend shows the earth's climate has warmed by approximately 0.36°F (0.2°C) per decade since the 1970s.

A Daunting Task

Back to reality. Myles Allen at Oxford has a vivid way of simplifying the scale of the task involved in preventing carbon levels rising above 450ppm. The modern world has been built on half a trillion tons of carbon. At present rates of increase we will burn the next half trillion tons in 40 years. The best guess is that that will result in a one-degree rise. There are, perhaps, four to five trillion tons of burnable carbon still in the Earth. But the maximum we can burn is half a trillion tons. In Copenhagen, therefore, the talks should be about allocating that half trillion as if it were a gigantic carbon cake. To make this work and ensure we don't burn more than that, Allen goes for a radical option. "It will only work," he says, "in the context of a plan to get emissions down to zero by the end of the century. So I think we need what none of the politicians seems prepared to acknowledge. A rationing system for putting carbon dioxide into the atmosphere is only a temporary measure; eventually the whole practice has to be banned."

This should give you vertigo. . . .

All Signs Point to Warming

Put it like this. Here are these scientists telling you probably your children and almost certainly your grandchildren are going to lead screwed-up lives thanks to our carbon emissions, and here are these economists arguing about the monetary value of their screwed-upness. Case closed.

Far stronger than all this are simple, empirical observations. Rapley points out that sea temperatures are rising exactly as predicted by the climate models. Climate change, more than over-fishing, has been found to be behind the fall in North Sea fish stocks. Arctic ice is melting faster than expected. And here's one fact that should give the most hardened bone-head pause: Arctic shipping lanes are to be re-opened. Summer sea ice in 2007 was 40% down on the average, and shipping companies are planning much faster routes between Europe and Asia using the Arctic Ocean. These guys are not exactly tree-huggers. And yet many denialists still insist on saying there's no problem with the Arctic melt.

One big general denialist argument is about climate models. These are fabulously complicated computer programmes that attempt to

Changes in Temperature, Sea Level and Northern Hemisphere Snow Cover

Data from the Intergovernmental Panel on Climate Change (IPCC) show that global average temperature and sea level have risen since the nineteenth century. The IPCC predicts temperatures will continue to rise throughout the twenty-first century.

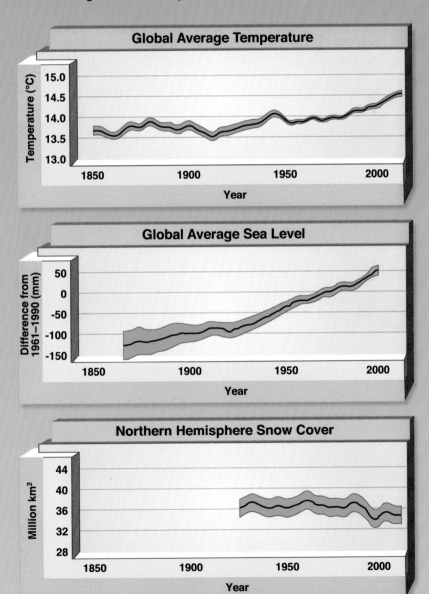

model the Earth's atmosphere. The number-crunching is so vast that Myles Allen has contracted it out to you and me. He began Climateprediction.net, which uses downtime on people's home computers to run climate simulations. Try it. You should. The idea is to cut the uncertainties in the models. And there are, no question, huge uncertainties. All complex systems are uncertain. But, for two closely related reasons, the denialists are wrong to claim this as an argument in their favour. First, empirical evidence either shows the models are right or, especially, in the case of Arctic ice, that they are understating the problem. [Scientist James] Lovelock, in particular, says this understatement has given us a model-based false sense of security. The disaster is coming much sooner than we thought.

EVALUATING THE AUTHOR'S ARGUMENTS:

Bryan Appleyard and Mike Maguire (author of the following viewpoint) disagree with each other over whether the planet is warming. In your opinion, which author makes the better argument? Why? List at least two pieces of evidence (quotations, statistics, facts, or statements of reasoning) that cause you to side with one author over the other.

The Planet Is Not Warming

Mike Maguire

"Eleven straight years of increasing CO_2 and we're still cooler than 1998."

Mike Maguire is a meteorologist. In the following viewpoint he challenges the notion that the planet is warming and that such warming is caused by humans. Maguire points out that although some of the twentieth century's years were marked by record warmth, other years and decades were very cool. Temperatures have been so mild, he says, that certain crops have enjoyed drought-free seasons and plentiful harvests. Maguire contends that the earth's temperature is very complicated and tied to multiple natural events and activities such as long-term natural cycles and solar activity. He accuses global warming believers of manipulating data and of drumming up baseless hysteria for their cause. Maguire concludes that climate science has been tainted by global warming activists who are more concerned with being right than reflecting the truth about the earth's naturally fluctuating temperature.

AS YOU READ, CONSIDER THE FOLLOWING QUESTIONS:

1. What happened to the earth's temperature between 1940 and 1970, according to Maguire?
2. What did the 2009 hurricane season prove to Maguire about the nature of weather?
3. Why does Maguire think it is absurd to treat carbon dioxide as pollution?

The hoax of man-made global warming is being exposed. Recent evidence of the doctoring of data by top climate scientists with political agendas to make it show warming that wasn't there and hide recent cooling is just the tip of the iceberg, one that is not melting as alarmists have been proclaiming. Let's review a few related facts.

With Warming Has Come Cooling

Temperatures have always fluctuated naturally on this planet. Looking back over the past 100 years, the earth warmed from 1900 to around 1940. There was global cooling after that until the late 1970s.

It warmed again in the 1980s and 1990s, with that warmth peaking in 1998. There has been no warming since then even as CO_2 [carbon dioxide] has increased during the entire period. Eleven straight years of increasing CO_2 and we're still cooler than 1998.

As of the 2009 growing season, the U.S. has now gone a record 21 straight years without a widespread drought in the Corn Belt. Soybean yields this year [2009] are easily a record. Corn yields were just shy of a record because it was actually too cool in the Upper Midwest. Climate models from man-made warming alarmists have consistently predicted increasing droughts along with yield-reducing excessive heat.

As a meteorologist who understands these models and appreciates our challenge to get the weather forecast right, it has amazed me that the public has been so easily bamboozled into believing the exaggerated 50-year cataclysmic climate forecasts.

Would you keep believing the same weatherman if he was wrong 11 forecasts in a row, then tried to sell you on his "long range" forecasts?

"Global Warming" Is the Result of Bias and Manipulation

The problem is that the source of these errant forecasts and flawed interpretations are biased scientists, working with leaders of groups with the same thing in mind. Their goal is to have a significant influence on governmental policy as it relates to regulating carbon dioxide. A key element to success has been manipulated data and propaganda.

Global warming has been twisted into a powerful issue that has attracted millions of loyal followers who believe the "debate is over," as Al Gore [the former vice president and environmentalist] stated. Realizing that the warming had stopped after 1998, they even changed the name to "climate change."

"Climategate," as it's now being called, is just evidence of what some of us scientists have known. We have been witnessing an unprecedented, coordinated campaign to prove the theory of Anthropogenic Global Warming and blame greenhouse gases using "whatever works" strategies.

The urgency to pass costly legislation has to do with shoving it through while many still have the illusion that it's worth the hefty cost and that the planet is still warming. Ironically, cap and trade in full force and doing what they claim it will to the earth's temperature would make a difference of only a tenth of 1 degree over the next 50 years. The natural cooking since 1998 is far greater than that.

Temperature Tends to Fluctuate

The 2009 hurricane season was quiet, the third in the last four years to be below preseason forecasts. This, after very active 2004, 2005 and 2008 seasons, shows more evidence of the natural variability. Atlantic basin activity is not determined by global temperatures, but from a natural 25-year cycle.

The sunspot count continues to be at the lowest level in a century. Looking back in the past, there appears to be a strong link between an inactive sun and a cooler earth. The sun is the source of incoming heat on this planet. It has cycles that we haven't been around long enough to study and understand clearly.

We do know with certainty that all of the many temperature fluctuations in the past were caused by natural cycles or events. These

natural cycles will continue with or without human beings. That's why temperatures have gone up and down the past 100 years, even while man-made CO_2 has gone up every year.

CO_2 Is Not Pollution

The biggest legitimate link involving CO_2 is with plants. We know that increasing CO_2 increases plant growth and crop yields. CO_2 is essential to all life forms on earth. Treating it as pollution is about as absurd as believing we can predict our climate 50 years from now. We also know that the warmer our planet has been in the past, the more life it supported. The most devastating blows to creatures on earth from temperatures came from cold.

Powerful evidence of life doing better because of increased CO_2 and warmth comes from digital satellite observations that were processed, refined and compared to changes of satellite-based maps of vegetation collected by the National Oceanic and Atmospheric Administration's series of AVHRR (Advanced Very High Resolution Radiometer) sensors. The digital satellite observations were processed into maps by NASA's [National Aeronautics and Space Administration's] Global Inventory Modeling and Mapping Studies project.

The time frame for this comprehensive study is significant. It studied the years of greatest warming this century. The scientists concluded: "Between 1982 and 1999, 25 percent of the Earth's vegetated area experienced increasing plant productivity."

They assumed that "increasing CO_2 caused plants to grow better" but "carbon dioxide fertilization couldn't be solely responsible for the change; climate change must be playing a role as well." Part of this was from more sunshine in the tropics and part of the increased plant productivity was from warmer temperatures in the high northern latitudes.

We Must Seek Out the Truth

I believe in reducing all forms of real pollution, recycling, conservation and developing renewable energy. I also believe strongly in telling the truth. The truth is that CO_2 is not pollution and that man did not cause much of the global warming that occurred in the last 100 years.

Don't believe the cleverly constructed presentations using distorted data from agenda-driven groups. They consider their hidden interests to be more important than the truth. They often use well-intentioned and credible people to help perpetrate the scam. Don't believe them.

We need to hold our policymakers accountable for their decisions, basing them on truth and the best interest of our country and planet. Don't believe me, either. Educate yourself on the subject, verify that everything stated here is the truth, and then believe it.

> **EVALUATING THE AUTHOR'S ARGUMENTS:**
>
> In this viewpoint Mike Maguire claims the planet is not significantly warming. What pieces of evidence does he provide to support this claim? List at least two quotations, statistics, facts, or statements of reasoning he offers to bolster his position. Did he convince you of his argument? Explain why or why not.

Viewpoint 3

Humans' Carbon Dioxide Emissions Are Causing Global Warming

National Academy of Sciences

"Most of the warming over the last several decades can be attributed to human activities that release carbon dioxide and other heat-trapping greenhouse gases into the atmosphere."

The following report was published by the National Academy of Sciences (NAS), a society of distinguished scholars who engage in scientific and engineering research. Congress created the NAS in 1863, during the Civil War. NAS argues that not only is the planet warming but also that humans are responsible for it. NAS explains that several different kinds of human activities—many of which are related to industry and development—have released large amounts of greenhouse gases into the atmosphere. The most threatening of these gases is carbon dioxide, which NAS says is causing the temperature to creep up, decade by decade, century by century. NAS warns that human-induced climate change and its consequences will last for many generations unless steps to curb greenhouse gas emissions are taken today.

1. How much warmer does NAS say was the first decade of the twenty-first century compared with the first decade of the twentieth century?
2. Name at least three human activities the author says have contributed to global warming.
3. What global temperature rise is associated with "extreme" climate change, according to the author?

Climate change is occurring, is caused largely by human activities, and poses significant risks for—and in many cases is already affecting—a broad range of human and natural systems.

Multiple Organizations Agree

This conclusion is based on a substantial array of scientific evidence, including recent work, and is consistent with the conclusions of recent assessments by the U.S. Global Change Research Program, the Intergovernmental Panel on Climate Change's Fourth Assessment Report, and other assessments of the state of scientific knowledge on climate change. Both our assessment . . . and these previous assessments place high or very high confidence in the following findings:

Earth is warming. Detailed observations of surface temperature assembled and analyzed by several different research groups show that the planet's average surface temperature was 1.4°F (0.8°C) warmer during the first decade of the 21st century than during the first decade of the 20th century, with the most pronounced warming over the past three decades. These data are corroborated by a variety of independent observations that indicate warming in other parts of the Earth system, including the cryosphere (snow- and ice-covered regions), the lower atmosphere, and the oceans.

Warming Is Due to Human Activity

Most of the warming over the last several decades can be attributed to human activities that release carbon dioxide (CO_2) and other heat-trapping green-house gases (GHGs) into the atmosphere. The burning of fossil fuels—coal, oil, and natural gas—for energy is the

A coal-fired power plant in China. According to the National Academy of Sciences, the burning of fossil fuels for energy is the single greatest contributor to global warming.

single largest human driver of climate change, but agriculture, forest clearing, and certain industrial activities also make significant contributions.

Natural climate variability leads to year-to-year and decade-to-decade fluctuations in temperature and other climate variables, as well as substantial regional differences, but cannot explain or offset the long-term warming trend. Global warming is closely associated with a broad spectrum of other changes, such as increases in the frequency of intense rainfall, decreases in Northern Hemisphere snow cover and Arctic sea ice, warmer and more frequent hot days and nights, rising sea levels, and widespread ocean acidification.

Human-induced climate change and its impacts will continue for many decades, and in some cases for many centuries. Individually and collectively, these changes pose risks for a wide range of human and environmental systems, including freshwater resources, the coastal environment, ecosystems, agriculture, fisheries, human health, and national security, among others. The ultimate magnitude of climate change and the severity of its impacts depend strongly on the actions that human societies take to respond to these risks.

Despite an international agreement to stabilize GHG concentrations "at levels that would avoid dangerous anthropogenic interference with the climate system," global emissions of CO_2 and several other GHGs continue to increase. Projections of future climate change, which are based on computer models of how the climate system would respond to different scenarios of future human activities, anticipate an additional warming of 2.0°F to 11.5°F (1.1°C to 6.4°C) over the 21st century. . . .

In general, it is reasonable to expect that the magnitude of future climate change and the severity of its impacts will be larger if actions are not taken to reduce GHG emissions and adapt to its impacts. . . .

An Uncertain Future

Climate change also poses challenges that set it apart from other risks with which people normally deal. For example, many climate change processes have considerable inertia and long time lags, so it is mainly future generations that will have to deal with the consequences (both positive and negative) of decisions made today. Also, rather than smooth and gradual climate shifts, there is the potential that the Earth system could cross tipping points or thresholds that result in abrupt changes. Some of the greatest risks posed by climate change are associated with these abrupt changes and other climate "surprises" (unexpected changes or impacts), yet the likelihood of such events is not well known. Moreover, there has been comparatively little research on the

FAST FACT

Researchers at Concordia University have calculated that the earth's temperature will rise 1.0–2.1°C (1.8–3.78°F) for every trillion tons of CO_2 emissions.

impacts that might be associated with "extreme" climate change—for example, the impacts that could be expected if global temperatures rise by 10°F (6°C) or more over the next century. Thus, while it seems clear that the Earth's future climate will be unlike the climate that ecosystems and human societies have become accustomed to during the last 10,000 years, the exact magnitude of future climate change and the nature of its impacts will always remain somewhat uncertain.

Americans Believe Global Warming Is Caused by Human Actions

The majority of Americans believe global warming is a man-made phenomenon, according to a poll taken by NBC News and the *Wall Street Journal*.

Participants were asked to choose one of two opposing statements as being closer to their own view. The first statement declares that human actions are a greater cause of global warming than natural forces, while the second statement declares that naturally occurring forces are the greater cause.

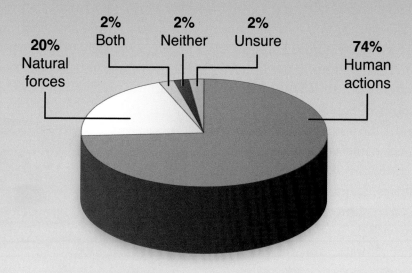

20%
Natural
forces

2%
Both

2%
Neither

2%
Unsure

74%
Human
actions

Taken from: NBC News/*Wall Street Journal* Poll, December 11–14, 2009.

Decision makers of all types, including businesses, governments, and individual citizens, are beginning to take actions to reduce the risks posed by climate change—including actions to limit its magnitude and actions to adapt to its impacts. Effective management of climate risks will require decision makers to take actions that are flexible and robust, to learn from new knowledge and experience, and to adjust future actions accordingly. The long time lags associated with climate change and the presence of differential vulnerabilities and capacities to respond to climate change likewise represent formidable management challenges. These challenges also have significant implications for the nation's climate science enterprise.

EVALUATING THE AUTHOR'S ARGUMENTS:

The National Academy of Sciences is one of the oldest and most authoritative scientific bodies in the United States. It was created by an Act of Congress that was signed by President Abraham Lincoln, which said its purpose was to "investigate, examine, experiment, and report upon any subject of science or art" whenever called upon to do so by any department of the government. Does knowing the history of the National Academy of Sciences influence your opinion of its argument on climate change? Why or why not? Explain your reasoning.

Humans' Carbon Dioxide Emissions Do Not Cause Any Significant Warming

David Evans

"Human carbon dioxide cannot possibly have caused the [warming] trend."

In the following viewpoint David Evans argues that carbon dioxide emissions from human activity do not significantly contribute to global warming. He discusses several inconsistencies and errors that he says have thrown climate science offtrack. One of these inconsistencies is how climate models work. Evans says climate models overestimate the effect carbon dioxide (CO_2) has on warming and moisture. He also says climate models fail to take into account very accurate data supplied by weather balloons, which show no evidence of CO_2-related warming. Evans suggests that climate change science has become big business—it keeps so many people employed and in power, there is little incentive for people who benefit from it to point out errors or inconsistencies. Evans concludes that CO_2 probably causes such minor warming that it is not worth changing human behavior in response.

Evans is a mathematician and engineer who served as a consultant to the Australian Greenhouse Office (now the Department of Climate Change) from 1999 to 2010, during which time he modeled Australia's carbon in plants, debris, mulch, soils, and forestry and agricultural products.

AS YOU READ, CONSIDER THE FOLLOWING QUESTIONS:
1. What, according to Evans, proves that climate models are fundamentally flawed?
2. According to Evans, by what degrees do "climate alarmists" keep lowering the temperature increases they expect per decade?
3. What does Evans say is true about the placement of 90 percent of official thermometers?

The debate about global warming has reached ridiculous proportions and is full of micro-thin half-truths and misunderstandings. I am a scientist who was on the carbon gravy train, understands the evidence, was once an alarmist, but am now a skeptic. Watching this issue unfold has been amusing but, lately, worrying. This issue is tearing society apart, making fools out of our politicians.

Let's set a few things straight.

Climate Change's Sordid History

The whole idea that carbon dioxide is the main cause of the recent global warming is based on a guess that was proved false by empirical evidence during the 1990s. But the gravy train was too big, with too many jobs, industries, trading profits, political careers, and the possibility of world government and total control riding on the outcome. So rather than admit they were wrong, the governments, and their tame climate scientists, now outrageously maintain the fiction that carbon dioxide is a dangerous pollutant.

Let's be perfectly clear. Carbon dioxide is a greenhouse gas, and other things being equal, the more carbon dioxide in the air, the warmer the planet. Every bit of carbon dioxide that we emit warms the planet. But the issue is not whether carbon dioxide warms the planet, but how much.

Most scientists, on both sides, also agree on how much a given increase in the level of carbon dioxide raises the planet's temperature, if just the extra carbon dioxide is considered. These calculations come from laboratory experiments; the basic physics have been well known for a century.

The disagreement comes about what happens next.

There Is Simply No Evidence That Extra CO_2 Causes Extreme Warming

The planet reacts to that extra carbon dioxide, which changes everything. Most critically, the extra warmth causes more water to evaporate from the oceans. But does the water hang around and increase the height of moist air in the atmosphere, or does it simply create more clouds and rain? Back in 1980, when the carbon dioxide theory started, no one knew. The alarmists guessed that it would increase the height of moist air around the planet, which would warm the planet even further, because the moist air is also a greenhouse gas.

This is the core idea of every official climate model: For each bit of warming due to carbon dioxide, they claim it ends up causing three bits of warming due to the extra moist air. The climate models amplify the carbon dioxide warming by a factor of three—so two-thirds of their projected warming is due to extra moist air (and other factors); only one-third is due to extra carbon dioxide.

That's the core of the issue. All the disagreements and misunderstandings spring from this. The alarmist case is based on this guess about moisture in the atmosphere, and there is simply no evidence for the amplification that is at the core of their alarmism.

Climate Models Are Flawed

Weather balloons had been measuring the atmosphere since the 1960s, many thousands of them every year. The climate models all predict that as the planet warms, a hot spot of moist air will develop over the tropics about 10 kilometres up, as the layer of moist air expands upwards into the cool dry air above. During the warming of the late 1970s, '80s and '90s, the weather balloons found no hot spot. None at all. Not even a small one. This evidence proves that the climate models are fundamentally flawed, that they greatly overestimate the temperature increases due to carbon dioxide.

This evidence first became clear around the mid-1990s.

At this point, official "climate science" stopped being a science. In science, empirical evidence always trumps theory, no matter how much you are in love with the theory. If theory and evidence disagree, real scientists scrap the theory. But official climate science ignored the crucial weather balloon evidence, and other subsequent evidence that backs it up, and instead clung to their carbon dioxide theory—that just happens to keep them in well-paying jobs with lavish research grants, and gives great political power to their government masters.

The Definition of "Worse" Keeps Changing

There are now several independent pieces of evidence showing that the earth responds to the warming due to extra carbon dioxide by dampening the warming. Every long-lived natural system behaves this way, counteracting any disturbance. Otherwise the system would be unstable. The climate system is no exception, and now we can prove it.

But the alarmists say the exact opposite, that the climate system amplifies any warming due to extra carbon dioxide, and is potentially unstable. It is no surprise that their predictions of planetary temperature made in 1988 to the U.S. Congress, and again in 1990, 1995, and 2001, have all proved much higher than reality.

They keep lowering the temperature increases they expect, from 0.30C per decade in 1990, to 0.20C per decade in 2001, and now 0.15C per decade—yet they have the gall to tell us "it's worse than expected." These people are not scientists. They overestimate the temperature increases due to carbon dioxide, selectively deny evidence, and now they conceal the truth.

Thermometer Trickery

One way they conceal is in the way they measure temperature.

The official thermometers are often located in the warm exhaust of air conditioning outlets, over hot tarmac at airports where they get blasts of hot air from jet engines, at waste-water plants where they get warmth from decomposing sewage, or in hot cities choked with cars and buildings. Global warming is measured in 10ths of a degree, so any extra heating nudge is important. In the United States, nearly 90% of official thermometers surveyed by volunteers violate official siting requirements that they not be too close to an artificial heating source.

Global temperature is also measured by satellites, which measure nearly the whole planet 24/7 without bias. The satellites say the hottest recent year was 1998, and that since 2001 the global temperature has levelled off. Why does official science track only the surface thermometer results and not mention the satellite results?

Human-Caused CO_2 Cannot Possibly Have Caused Recent Warming

The Earth has been in a warming trend since the depth of the Little Ice Age around 1680. Human emissions of carbon dioxide were negligible before 1850 and have nearly all come after the Second World War, so human carbon dioxide cannot possibly have caused the trend. Within the trend, the Pacific Decadal Oscillation causes alternating global warming and cooling for 25 to 30 years at a go in each direction. We have just finished a warming phase, so expect mild global cooling for the next two decades.

We are now at an extraordinary juncture. Official climate science, which is funded and directed entirely by government, promotes a

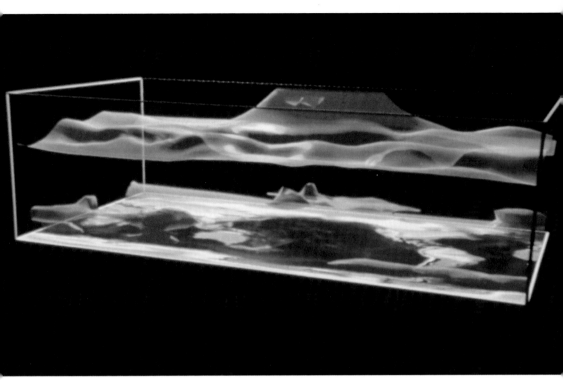

This computer-generated model is used to study temperature and soil moisture differences due to global warming. Global warming detractors say the climate models contain insufficient or erroneous data.

theory that is based on a guess about moist air that is now a known falsehood. Governments gleefully accept their advice, because the only ways to curb emissions are to impose taxes and extend government control over all energy use. And to curb emissions on a world scale might even lead to world government—how exciting for the political class!

Even if we stopped emitting all carbon dioxide tomorrow, completely shut up shop and went back to the Stone Age, according to the official government climate models it would be cooler in 2050 by about 0.015 degrees. But their models exaggerate 10-fold—in fact our sacrifices would make the planet in 2050 a mere 0.0015 degrees cooler!

Finally, to those who still believe the planet is in danger from our carbon dioxide emissions: Sorry, but you've been had. Yes, carbon dioxide is a cause of global warming, but it's so minor it's not worth doing much about.

EVALUATING THE AUTHOR'S ARGUMENTS:

To make his argument, David Evans says climate models that predict global warming are critically flawed. How do you think the other authors in this chapter would respond to this suggestion? After reading all of the viewpoints, write one or two sentences on what you think each author might say about the accuracy of climate models. Then, state your opinion. Do you trust such models? Do you think they accurately predict global warming, or not? Why? Cite evidence from at least one text that swayed you.

Chapter 2

Does Global Warming Pose a Serious Threat?

Melting icebergs in Antarctica are seen in 2007. Some argue that global warming is responsible for rapid melting.

Viewpoint

1

The Effects of Global Warming Will Be Catastrophic

"This is the first time that scientists have said that society is now on a path to meet it [a 6°C rise in global temperature]."

Steve Connor and Michael McCarthy

In the following viewpoint Steve Connor and Michael McCarthy argue that the world is now on course for the worst-case climate change scenario. Scientists predict global temperatures will rise by 6°C by the end of the century, which will have catastrophic consequences, insist Connor and McCarthy. They explain that a rise in temperature of this magnitude will propel the planet into an "extreme greenhouse state not seen for nearly 100 million years," resulting in mass extinctions of almost all life. The abrupt temperature climb would melt ice caps, render the tropics too hot to grow crops, and cause fierce competition for habitable areas.

Steve Connor is the science editor and Michael McCarthy is the environment editor for the *Independent*.

1. Why, according to Connor and McCarthy, do scientists say the world is headed for a temperature rise of 6°C?
2. What failure of Earth's natural ability, according to the authors, have scientists detected for the first time?
3. Why would a temperature climb of 6°C cause mass extinctions, according to the Connor and McCarthy?

The world is now firmly on course for the worst-case scenario in terms of climate change, with average global temperatures rising by up to 6C [6°C] by the end of the century, leading scientists said yesterday. Such a rise—which would be much higher nearer the poles—would have cataclysmic and irreversible consequences for the Earth, making large parts of the planet uninhabitable and threatening the basis of human civilisation.

We are headed for it, the scientists said, because the carbon dioxide emissions from industry, transport and deforestation which are responsible for warming the atmosphere have increased dramatically since 2002, in a way which no one anticipated, and are now running at treble the annual rate of the 1990s.

This means that the most extreme scenario envisaged in the last report from the [United Nations'] UN Intergovernmental Panel on Climate Change, published in 2007, is now the one for which society is set, according to the 31 researchers from seven countries involved in the Global Carbon Project.

Although the 6C rise and its potential disastrous effects have been speculated upon before, this is the first time that scientists have said that society is now on a path to meet it. . . .

[A serious deal for cutting carbon emissions, including in the US and China,] cannot come too soon, to judge by the results of the Global Carbon Project study, led by Professor Corinne Le Quere, of the University of East Anglia and the British Antarctic Survey, which found that there has been a 29 per cent increase in global CO_2 emissions from fossil fuel between 2000 and 2008, the last year for which figures are available.

Increases in Emissions

On average, the researchers found, there was an annual increase in emissions of just over 3 per cent during the period, compared with an annual increase of 1 per cent between 1990 and 2000. Almost all of the increase this decade occurred after 2000 and resulted from the boom in the Chinese economy. . . .

In total, CO_2 emissions from the burning of fossil fuels have increased by 41 per cent between 1990 and 2008, yet global emissions in 1990 are the reference level set by the Kyoto Protocol, which countries are trying to fall below in terms of their own emissions.

The 6C rise now being anticipated is in stark contrast to the C rise at which all international climate policy, including that of Britain and the EU [European Union], hopes to stabilise the warming—two degrees being seen as the threshold of climate change which is dangerous for society and the natural world. . . .

Professor Le Quere said, . . . "The Copenhagen conference next month is in my opinion the last chance to stabilise climate at C above pre-industrial levels in a smooth and organised way," she said.

"If the agreement is too weak, or the commitments not respected, it is not 2.5C or 3C we will get: it's 5C or 6C—that is the path we're on. The timescales here are extremely tight for what is needed to stabilise the climate at C," she said.

Meanwhile, the scientists have for the first time detected a failure of the Earth's natural ability to absorb man-made carbon dioxide released into the air.

> ## FAST FACT
>
> According to the Intergovernmental Panel on Climate Change (IPCC), by 2100 greenhouse gas levels could rise to 710–1130 parts per million (ppm) and global temperatures could rise by an average of 6.4°C (11.5°F). In 2009 the British Met Office confirmed this catastrophic scenario; unchecked global warming is on track for a 4°C (7.2°F) rise by 2060 that would threaten the water supply of half the world's population, wipe out up to half the world's plant and animal species, and submerge low coastal regions.

Dhaka, the capital of Bangladesh, was partially submerged by flooding in 1988. A one-foot rise in sea level would affect more than thirteen thousand miles and create 100 million refugees.

"Carbon Sinks"

They found significant evidence that more man-made CO_2 is staying in the atmosphere to exacerbate the greenhouse effect because the natural "carbon sinks" that have absorbed it over previous decades on land and sea are beginning to fail, possibly as a result of rising global temperatures.

The amount of CO_2 that has remained in the atmosphere as a result has increased from about 40 per cent in 1990 to 45 per cent in 2008. This suggests that the sinks are beginning to fail, they said.

Professor Le Quere emphasised that there are still many uncertainties over carbon sinks, such as the ability of the oceans to absorb dissolved CO_2, but all the evidence suggests that there is now a cycle of "positive feedbacks", whereby rising carbon dioxide emissions are leading to rising temperatures and a corresponding rise in carbon dioxide in the atmosphere.

"Our understanding at the moment in the computer models we have used—and they are state of the art—suggests that carbon-cycle climate feedback has already kicked in," she said.

"These models, if you project them on into the century, show quite large feedbacks, with climate amplifying global warming by between 5 per cent and 30 per cent. There are still large uncertainties, but this is carbon-cycle climate feedback that has already started," she said.

The study also found that, for the first time since the 1960s, the burning of coal has overtaken the burning of oil as the major source of carbon-dioxide emissions produced by fossil fuels.

Much of this coal was burned by China in producing goods sold to the West—the scientists estimate that 45 per cent of Chinese emissions resulted from making products traded overseas. . . .

6°C Rise: The Consequences

If two degrees is generally accepted as the threshold of dangerous climate change, it is clear that a rise of six degrees in global average temperatures must be very dangerous indeed, writes Michael McCarthy. Just how dangerous was signalled in 2007 by the science writer Mark Lynas, who combed all the available scientific research to construct a picture of a world with temperatures three times higher than the danger limit.

His verdict was that a rise in temperatures of this magnitude "would catapult the planet into an extreme greenhouse state not seen for nearly 100 million years, when dinosaurs grazed on polar rainforests and deserts reached into the heart of Europe".

He said: "It would cause a mass extinction of almost all life and probably reduce humanity to a few struggling groups of embattled survivors clinging to life near the poles."

Very few species could adapt in time to the abruptness of the transition, he suggested. "With the tropics too hot to grow crops, and the sub-tropics too dry, billions of people would find themselves in areas of the planet which are essentially uninhabitable. This would probably even include southern Europe, as the Sahara desert crosses the Mediterranean.

"As the ice-caps melt, hundreds of millions will also be forced to move inland due to rapidly-rising seas. As world food supplies crash, the higher mid-latitude and sub-polar regions would become fiercely-contested refuges.

"The British Isles, indeed, might become one of the most desirable pieces of real estate on the planet. But, with a couple of billion people knocking on our door, things might quickly turn rather ugly."

The Effects of Global Warming Will Not Be Catastrophic

Bjorn Lomborg, interviewed by Gene Epstein

"There is much more sizzle in saying the world is going to come to an end than there is to saying, it is a bit of a problem and we need to fix it smartly, but that is it."

Bjorn Lomborg is a Danish author known for his suspicion of global warming hysteria. In the following viewpoint he argues that global warming advocates exaggerate the threats from global temperature rise. For example, he acknowledges that sea levels might rise as a result of global warming but says if they do, there will not be much resulting damage. Likewise, changes to the ocean could benefit marine life, and if they do not, Lomborg says humans can survive and thrive despite such losses. Lomborg says many cities have already responded to challenges posed by climate change, and done so reasonably and with ease. In his opinion, there is no reason to think that global warming will wreak any havoc with which humanity cannot cope. Lomborg concludes that environmentalists trade in fear and hysteria, both of which impede innovative thinking and smart decision making on problems as complicated as global warming.

Lomborg is the author of the book *The Skeptical Environmentalist.*

AS YOU READ, CONSIDER THE FOLLOWING QUESTIONS:
1. How many inches or feet does Lomborg say the seas are expected to rise by 2100?
2. How does Lomborg say the island of Manhattan could protect itself from dramatic sea level rise?
3. About how many deaths per year are heat-related, according to Lomborg? How many are cold-related?

[B arron's:] *Isn't it smart to prevent global warming as soon as possible—to avoid seeing Manhattan under 20 feet of water in ten years?*

[Bjorn Lomborg:] That makes for vivid imagery, but it isn't what the science is telling us. According to the thousands of scientists the U.N. [United Nations] asked to evaluate the data, the sea-level rise between now and 2100 will be somewhere between six inches and two feet—not 20 feet—with most estimates around one foot. Now, we have already seen a foot of sea-level rise over the last 150 years, so it will be a bit faster by 2100. But it certainly gives you perspective. Was the 20th century marked particularly by the fact that the sea level rose? Well, there were two world wars, the suffrage of women, the internal-combustion engine, the IT [information technology] revolution—and the sea level rose. Let's hope the 21st century sees no world wars, but do you think the sea-level rise will be any more important? That doesn't mean it isn't a problem, but it's a problem we can deal with.

Extreme Sea Level Rise Is Not Something to Worry About in Most Cases

New York City actually has more land mass than it used to, even though the sea level rose. Holland has been way below sea level for centuries, on the order of 10 to 12 feet below sea level for about 60% of the Dutch, and with no visible decrease in their quality of life. Take the Republic of Maldives, an island country consisting of a group of atolls. The sea level rise would mean a 77% land-loss for the Maldives, worth more than that country's entire gross domestic product [GDP]. But protection against the sea will cost only about 0.4% of GDP, which makes almost every square foot worth saving.

And if it really were true that Manhattan will be 20 feet underwater in 10 years, there would be no time to reverse global warming anyway. Once Manhattanites witness the first three feet of sea-level rise in three years, the only sane thing would be to build dikes. And let's remember that you don't have to see the dikes. The Dutch don't normally see their dikes or feel surrounded by them. Not that many of the scientists who have looked at the data expect that kind of catastrophe.

We Can Cope with Temperature Rises

But aren't there certain irreversible catastrophes from global warming that could truly do us in?

The United Nations science consensus expects temperature increases of three to seven degrees Fahrenheit by the end of the century, which the world can deal with, especially if the world is allowed to grow richer between now and then. And while it is important to admit that there is no guaranteeing the future, catastrophe from global warming is just one of many imaginable catastrophes. There are plenty of other scary scenarios out there in the world, certainly including the fact that we could see a new ice age. And if we allow ourselves to say anything and everything could happen, then we should ask how we can best protect ourselves against all these different catastrophes that could come along. We do know that rich, well-structured, robust societies deal much better with catastrophe than weak, poorly structured societies. We also know the way to build those societies isn't to cripple the global economy by forcing it off fossil fuels before viable alternatives are available.

Meanwhile, three-fourths of the world's people live in abject poverty, while some sit and fret about the possible end of the world in 100 years. For too many of those others, the world ends tomorrow.

Cold Is More Dangerous than Heat

You have pointed out that some effects of global warming might be the reverse of catastrophic by saving lives on balance.

Yes. Take deaths caused by temperature extremes—a good example of how we get very biased reporting. Everybody says when temperatures rise, you are going to get more heat waves and therefore you are going to get more heat deaths. That is absolutely true. But you also have to remember that as temperatures rise, you are also going to get fewer cold waves. While warming will mean about 400,000 more heat-related deaths globally, it will mean 1.8 million fewer cold-related deaths, according to the only peer-reviewed global estimate, published in *Ecological Economics*, something that is rarely reported. That is partly because warming will disproportionately cause warmer winters rather than hotter summers.

And when it comes to heat deaths, cutting carbon emissions is an incredibly costly and ineffective way to help people who will die more from heat. If we care about heat deaths we should make sure that people don't get so hot in the summer in the heat waves. If we plant more trees, if we make more water and air-conditioning available, if

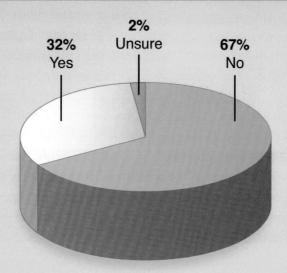

Americans Do Not See a Threat from Global Warming in Their Lifetimes

Question: "Do you think global warming will pose a serious threat to you or your way of life in your lifetime?"

32% Yes

2% Unsure

67% No

Taken from: Gallup Poll, March 4–7, 2010.

we maintain more light surfaces—for instance, by painting the tarmac white—we could actually save far more lives from extremes of heat much faster and more cheaply.

Some Climate Change Consequences Will Have Little Effect on Humans

What about the damage to sea life from ocean acidification due to carbon dioxide?

There is some validity to that concern. But the claim that this could be catastrophic for marine life seems greatly exaggerated, since we know there have been vastly higher carbon-dioxide levels in the atmosphere some 50 to 500 million years ago, at a time when the ocean was very rich in marine life. And even if we imagine such a

Author Bjorn Lomborg of Denmark has been an outspoken critic of advocates of global warming, saying they exaggerate the effects of rising sea levels.

catastrophe could happen, let's get a grip on its human impact. We get about 1% of our calories from the seas and about 5% of our protein. We mainly depend on the land for our food, and land-based productivity will be growing dramatically.

Why is it that what you are saying about global warming is so contradictory to everything else that most people read, see and hear in the media?

Well, there are several reasons. It is partly because they don't read the U.N. reports, which on many of these issues confirm what I am saying very clearly. And since the sensational always goes over better than the merely sensible, stories in the media play into the stereotype of global warming. There is much more sizzle in saying the world is going to come to an end than there is to saying, it is a bit of a problem and we need to fix it smartly, but that is it. The scary stories also appeal to the visceral hatred of materialism harbored by many, even when they are materialist in their own habits.

It is much easier to find a real person who died in the heat wave in 2003 in Paris, and tell that story. It is much harder to tell a compelling story about a person who didn't die from cold in Paris in the winter of 2003. So it is often much easier to show all the problems from global warming, and very much harder to show all the distributed benefits from pursuing more sensible policies.

> ## FAST FACT
>
> Population biologist Camille Parmesan reported in a March 2011 *Nature* interview that, consistent with a warming world, spring now begins two weeks earlier. According to Parmesan, plants and animals are already adapting to climate change: Almost two-thirds of species, including birds, frogs, butterflies, and trees, are breeding or blooming earlier, and more than 50 percent are changing where they live.

We Must Make Smart, Simple Choices

Finally, politicians obviously garner a lot of support by saying we want to save the planet much more than they garner support if they talk about making smart, simple policies that might also be politically difficult to get through. Essentially, they get to promise they are going to cut emissions in 2020 or 2050—when they are not going to be politicians any longer.

[Former vice president and environmentalist] Al Gore talks about global warming as our generational mission. He asks how we want to be remembered by our kids and grandkids. Well, why would anyone want to be remembered for having spent $180 billion to do virtually no good a hundred years from now, when less than half that sum could fix virtually all major problems today? With better information, most of us would have no difficulty choosing how we want to be remembered.

EVALUATING THE AUTHOR'S ARGUMENTS:

Bjorn Lomborg contends that most challenges posed by global warming have a reasonable and relatively simple solution. How do you think the other authors in this chapter would respond to this claim? Write one or two sentences for each author. Then, state your position on the matter. Quote from the texts you have read in your answer.

Global Warming Threatens Crop Growth

Kent Garber

"A rise in temperature—even as little as 1 degree Celsius—could cause many plantings to fail."

In the following viewpoint Kent Garber explains the ways in which increased global temperatures will threaten the global food supply. He says as temperatures rise, growing seasons will become hotter and longer. This will spur the growth of weeds and insects and damage or reduce the yields of particularly heat-sensitive crops. Hotter, longer summers will also trigger droughts and outbreaks of disease, he maintains, which will be particularly damaging to crops. Increased population and demand for food will further stress the food system, Garber warns. He concludes that global warming will have dramatic consequences on the world's crops and actions must be taken to prevent as much damage as possible.

Garber is a reporter for *US News and World Report*, where this viewpoint was originally published.

AS YOU READ, CONSIDER THE FOLLOWING QUESTIONS:
1. What has aided the spread of the invasive kudzu vine, according to Garber?
2. What effect do high ozone levels have on soybean, wheat, and peanut crop yields, according to a study?
3. What problems does Garber say come with longer growing seasons?

The global food supply, as recent events have shown all too clearly, is threatened by many problems. Some of them are man-made; some are natural. The natural ones tend to be obvious—droughts, floods, hurricanes, earthquakes—and, in the past year alone [2008], they have been notably devastating. Searing droughts in Australia and central Europe have squandered wheat supplies; more recently, Cyclone Nargis destroyed rice stocks for millions of people in Myanmar.

Historically, the damage to food supplies by bad weather has been regarded as fleeting: catastrophic in the short term but ultimately remitting. Droughts ease, floodwaters recede, and farmers replant their crops. But as a new government report indicates, such views are increasingly narrow and outdated, in that they fail to acknowledge the creeping reach of global climate change.

Global Warming Will Hurt Crops

The report, released Tuesday [May 27, 2008], offers one of the most comprehensive looks yet at the impact that climate change is expected to have on U.S. agriculture over the next several decades. Not surprisingly, the prognosis is grim. Temperatures in the United States, scientists say, will rise on average by about 1.2 degrees Celsius by 2040, with carbon dioxide levels up more than 15 percent. The consequences for American-grown food, the report finds, will most likely be far-reaching: Some crop yields are predicted to drop; growing seasons will get longer and use more water; weeds and shrubs will grow faster and spread into new territory, some of it arable farmland; and insect and crop disease outbreaks will become more frequent.

The new report, which was produced by more than a dozen agencies over multiple years and reflects the findings of more than 1,000 scientific studies, offers only predictions, but the predictions reflect a high degree of confidence. In a sense, there is a vein of fatalism among most scientists about what will happen in the next few decades. Government actions, they say, may alter the trajectory of climate change 50 to 100 years from now, but the fate of climate change in the short term has been largely shaped by past behavior, by carbon already released into the atmosphere. The question now is the extent of its impact.

Heat-Sensitive Crops Will Suffer

Some agricultural changes are already observable. In the central Great Plains, in states known for their grassy prairies and sprawling row crops, there are new neighbors: trees and large shrubs, often clustering in islands in the middle of fields. In the Southwest, perennial grasses have been largely pushed out by mesquite bushes, those long-rooted staples of the desert. And the invasive kudzu vine, formerly a nuisance only to the South, has advanced steadily northward, forming a staggered line stretching from Connecticut to Illinois. Human practices in all three cases have abetted the turnover, but climate change, scientists say, has been a primary driver, as invasive species reproduce more quickly and expand into areas once deemed too cold for their survival. In turn, high-quality pastureland, once ideal for livestock grazing, has become poor-quality brush, and farmland faces competitors for space.

> **FAST FACT**
>
> A 2011 study by Stanford researcher David Lobell concludes that a rise in average temperature of only 1°C will reduce corn crop yields across two-thirds of the maize-growing region of Africa. If temperature rise is accompanied by drought, Lobell predicts crop yields will be reduced by 1.7 percent per day for every day whose peak temperature is above 86°F (30°C).

In the next 30 years these problems will very likely expand and multiply, as an already taxed food system faces threats on multiple fronts. A rise in temperature—even as little as 1 degree Celsius—could cause many plantings to fail, the report indicates, since pollen and seeds

Decrease in Crop Yields per Degree of Warming

A National Research Council study found that crops of maize, soybeans, rice, and wheat all suffered in warmer weather, producing less usable product per degree of warming.

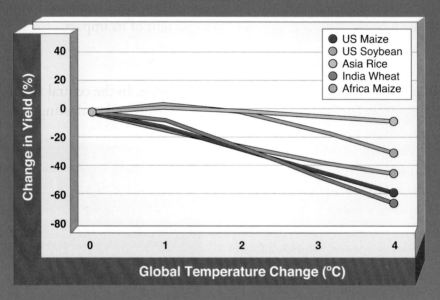

Taken from: National Research Council. "Climate Stabilization Targets: Emissions, Concentrations, and Impacts Over Decades to Millennia," 2011.

are sensitive to slight temperature changes. Yields of corn and rice are expected to decline slightly. Heat-sensitive fruits and vegetables, such as tomatoes, will most likely suffer. Some of the potential damage will be blunted by higher carbon dioxide levels; soybean yields, for instance, will probably improve, because soybeans (and several other crops) thrive from higher carbon inputs. But if temperatures keep rising, the balance will ultimately tip: At some extreme temperature, cells stop dividing, and pollen dies.

The Threat from Ozone, Insects, and Disease

High ozone levels, which have risen sixfold in the United States in the past century and are expected to rise further, will suppress yields as well. In fact, ozone levels are already extremely high in the eastern and midwestern regions of the country, rivaled globally only by eastern China (no model of air quality, to be sure) and parts of western Europe. One recent study, for instance, found that high ozone levels significantly suppress yields of soybean, wheat, and peanuts in the Midwest.

Eventually, the effects of climate change, far from being limited to individual plants, could percolate throughout entire ecosystems. If springs become warmer, as predicted, the crop-growing season will expand. Insects and pests, thriving in warmer winters, will reproduce more frequently and spread more rapidly. Many, in fact, are proliferating already, as reflected in reports of abnormally high rates of disease outbreaks in the western half of the United States. Higher temperatures also are usually accompanied by declining rainfall, threatening to slowly transform once lush areas into arid expanses. At the same time, droughts and heavy isolated rainfalls could become more numerous.

For all the criticism that has been piled upon the $300 billion farm bill that Congress recently passed over President [George W.] Bush's veto, the bill does include many provisions that pertain directly to concerns cited in the new report. Fruit and vegetable growers, for instance, will receive millions of dollars of new funding for research on pest and disease resistance.

EVALUATING THE AUTHOR'S ARGUMENTS:

In this viewpoint Kent Garber uses facts, statistics, examples, and reasoning to make his argument that global warming will hurt crops. He does not, however, use any quotations to support his point. If you were to rewrite this article and insert quotations, what authorities might you quote from? Where would you place them, and why?

Global Warming Is Creating Perfect Crop Conditions

James Taylor

"While alarmists cry about global warming and crop devastation, consumers in the real world have never had such an abundance of plenty."

In the following viewpoint James Taylor argues that global warming does not threaten crops—on the contrary, he says increased temperatures have improved growing conditions and crop yields and predicts this pattern will continue as temperatures rise. He says that warmer temperatures and excess carbon dioxide (CO_2) increase soil quality, extend growing seasons, and contribute to wetter conditions, all of which boost crop yields. He lists numerous crops that have enjoyed record yields in recent years and says that previously drought- and famine-stricken regions have begun to benefit from global warming–related phenomena. He concludes that global warming is heralding in a golden age of agriculture that will help alleviate food scarcity and hunger.

James Taylor, "Global Warming Is Creating Perfect Crop Conditions," *Forbes,* March 23, 2011. Reprinted by Permission of Forbes Media LLC 2011. This article has been slightly modified from its original format for educational purposes.

Taylor is the managing editor of *Environment & Climate News* and a senior fellow for the Heartland Institute, where he focuses on environmental issues. He writes a regular column for *Forbes* magazine, where this viewpoint was originally published. This article has been slightly modified from its original format for educational purposes.

AS YOU READ, CONSIDER THE FOLLOWING QUESTIONS:
1. Name at least five crops Taylor says have enjoyed record per-acre yields in the five years leading up to this article.
2. Since what year does Taylor say global grain harvests have nearly tripled?
3. What did a January 2007 study published in the journal *Geology* find about the rainfall in Africa, as reported by Taylor?

The news media are flush with stories this week [March 2011] claiming global warming is crushing global crop production. According to the media, global warming is putting the hurt on two of our favorite indulgences—coffee and beer. For the more globally conscious (or less caffeinated/less inebriated) among us, the media are also focusing attention on an alleged African corn crisis. A look at facts rather than alarmist speculation, however, shows global warming is strongly benefiting nearly all global crops, including coffee, beer barley, and African corn.

Global Warming Improves Crop Production

Without a doubt, global warming is affecting global crop production. The tremendous improvement in global crop production and worldwide growing conditions during recent decades is one of the most important yet least reported news events of our time. As the earth continues to recover from the abnormally cold conditions of the centuries-long Little Ice Age, warmer temperatures, improving soil moisture, and more abundant atmospheric carbon dioxide have helped bring about a golden age for global agricultural production.

During the past decade, which alarmists claim is the warmest in recent history, record per-acre yields have been recorded for nearly every important U.S. crop. During the past five years alone, according to the U.S. Department of Agriculture, record per-acre yields have been registered for barley, beans, canola, corn, cotton, flaxseed, oats, peanuts, potatoes, rice, sorghum, soybeans, sugarbeets, sunflowers, and wheat.

Crop Yields Have Soared

Global crop yields have also registered spectacular growth as global temperatures have warmed. Global grain harvests have nearly tripled since 1961. As is the case in the U.S., nearly every important global crop has attained record productivity during the past five years, including the Big Three: corn, rice, and wheat crops.

Indeed, while the media claim global warming is threatening our morning coffee, farmers are preparing to harvest a record global coffee crop. While the media claim global warming is jeopardizing our beer bellies by harming barley production, U.S. farmers in 2009 netted their highest ever barley yield per acre. Claims that global warming is harming African corn production are the most ridiculous of all.

During the past decade, African nations have registered record harvests in a variety of crops, including corn and rice. Moreover, the modestly warming climate is stimulating more frequent and abundant rainfall which, together with more atmospheric carbon dioxide, is greening the African continent.

FAST FACT

Russia's growing season will be longer, and the defrosted land area suitable for agriculture will increase by up to 33 million hectares (81.5 million acres) by 2050 and 46 million hectares (113.7 million acres) by 2150.

Higher Temperatures Help Rainfall

A March 2009 study in the peer-reviewed *Biogeosciences* reported the Sahel region of the southern Sahara Desert was growing greener, sending the Sahara desert into retreat. According to the study, "satellite sensors have recently shown that much of the region has experienced significant increases in photosynthetic activity since the early 1980s." According to the study, more abundant rainfall was the most likely

Crops Love Carbon Dioxide

Experiments by the Center for the Study of Carbon Dioxide and Global Change found that many of the world's most important crops responded positively when exposed to increased levels of carbon dioxide (CO_2)— an increase of 300 parts per million. Some crops even doubled their yields. Some people have used this data to argue global warming will improve crop conditions and help alleviate world hunger.

Crop	% Increase, Dry Weight	Crop	% Increase, Dry Weight
Pineapples	5.0%	Sesame seed	43.3%
Millet	13.5%	Oranges	44.1%
Onions, dry	20.0%	Apples	44.2%
Sorghum	20.7%	Apricots	44.2%
Maize	21.3%	Avocados	44.2%
Watermelons	23.1%	Bananas	44.2%
Spinach	24.3%	Cashew nuts, with shell	44.2%
Chillies and peppers, green	25.0%	Cocoa beans	44.2%
Peaches and nectarines	27.8%	Coconuts	44.2%
Tangerines, mandarins	29.5%	Dates	44.2%
Potatoes	31.4%	Figs	44.2%
Wheat	31.9%	Hazelnuts, with shell	44.2%
Okra	32.0%	Kiwi fruit	44.2%
Peas, dry	33.3%	Oil palm fruit	44.2%
Peas, green	33.3%	Papayas	44.2%
Sweet potatoes	33.7%	Pears	44.2%
Sugar cane	34.0%	Persimmons	44.2%
Oats	34.8%	Pistachios	44.2%
Olives	35.2%	Plantains	44.2%
Lettuce and chicory	35.6%	Plums and sloes	44.2%
Rice	35.7%	Tea	44.2%
Mangoes, mangosteens, guavas	36.0%	Broad beans, horse beans, dry	46.3%
Rye	37.3%	Soybeans	46.5%
Triticale	37.3%	Cucumbers and gherkins	50.2%
Tomatoes	37.4%	Garlic	54.1%
Sunflower seed	37.5%	Yams	54.1%
Barley	38.9%	Cherries	56.2%
Eggplants (aubergines)	41.0%	Beans, green	57.7%
Grapefruit (inc. pomelos)	41.1%	Seed cotton	60.6%
Lemons and limes	41.1%	Beans, dry	61.7%
Pumpkins, squash, and gourds	41.5%	Lentils	61.7%
Cabbages and other brassicas	42.0%	Sugar beet	66.3%
Cauliflowers and broccoli	42.0%	Grapes	68.2%
Rapeseed	42.0%	Carrots and turnips	77.8%
Artichokes	43.3%	Pigeon peas	109.5%
Asparagus	43.3%	Onions, green	135.0%
Jute	43.3%	Coffee, green	175.5%

Taken from: Center for the Study of Carbon Dioxide and Global Change, 2011.

cause, more than compensating for higher evaporation rates due to modestly rising temperatures.

A July 2009 *National Geographic News* article confirmed the *Biogeosciences* study. "Emerging evidence is painting a very different scenario, one in which rising temperatures could benefit millions of Africans in the driest parts of the continent," *National Geographic News* reported.

"Scientists are now seeing signals that the Sahara desert and surrounding regions are greening due to increasing rainfall. If sustained, these rains could revitalize drought-ravaged regions, reclaiming them for farming communities," *National Geographic News* explained. "This desert-shrinking trend is supported by climate models, which predict a return to conditions that turned the Sahara into a lush savanna some 12,000 years ago," the article noted.

Global Warming Contributes to an Abundance of Plenty

A January 2007 study in the peer-reviewed science journal *Geology* explained the greening of Africa in a longer-term context. According to the study, much of Africa is currently "experiencing an unusually prolonged period of stable, wet conditions in comparison to previous centuries of the past millennium. . . . The patterns and variability of 20th century rainfall in central Africa have been unusually conducive to human welfare in the context of the past 1400 years."

While alarmists cry about global warming and crop devastation, consumers in the real world have never had such an abundance of plenty.

> **EVALUATING THE AUTHOR'S ARGUMENTS:**
>
> James Taylor and Kent Garber (author of the previous viewpoint) come to drastically different conclusions on whether global warming will help or hurt crops. In your opinion, which author presented better evidence, and with whom do you ultimately agree? List at least one piece of evidence that swayed you.

Global Warming Is Causing Extreme Weather

"Several types of extreme weather events have occurred more frequently or with greater intensity in recent years. Global warming may drive changes in the frequency, timing, location or severity of such events."

Environment New Jersey Research & Policy Center

Environment New Jersey Research & Policy Center is an environmental organization dedicated to protecting air, water, and open spaces. In the following viewpoint the author warns that global warming is contributing to extreme weather events such as hurricanes, droughts, wildfires, and heat waves. It catalogues the increased frequency of these events and connects their occurrence to a rise in global temperatures. The author explains that severe weather costs lives and billions of dollars in damage. It threatens infrastructure, farmland, crop production, wildlife, and urban spaces. The viewpoint concludes that the United States and other countries should take all possible steps to prevent global warming so that they can avoid the risks from extreme weather.

Environment America Research & Policy Center, "Executive Summary," in *Global Warming and Extreme Weather: The Science, the Forecasts, and the Impacts on America,* Environment New Jersey Research & Policy Center, 2010, pp. 1–4.

AS YOU READ, CONSIDER THE FOLLOWING QUESTIONS:
1. What does the author predict will happen to category four and five hurricanes in the Atlantic over the course of the next century?
2. How many people in the mid-Atlantic region does the author say would be threatened by a one-meter rise in sea level?
3. By what percent did the number of heavy precipitation events increase in the United States between 1948 and 2006, according to the viewpoint?

Patterns of extreme weather are changing in the United States, and climate science predicts that further changes are in store. Extreme weather events lead to billions of dollars in economic damage and loss of life each year. Scientists project that global warming could affect the frequency, timing, location and severity of many types of extreme weather events in the decades to come.

Over the last five years, science has continued to make progress in exploring the connections between global warming and extreme weather. Meanwhile, the United States has experienced a string of extreme events—including massive floods in the Midwest, Tennessee and Northeast, intense hurricanes in Florida and along the Gulf Coast, drought and wildfire in the Southeast and Southwest—that serve as a reminder of the damage that extreme weather can cause to people, the economy and the environment. . . .

To protect the nation from the damage to property and ecosystems that results from changes in extreme weather patterns—as well as other consequences of global warming—the United States must move quickly to reduce emissions of global warming pollutants.

Scientists Agree That Humans Are Causing Warming

The worldwide scientific consensus that the earth is warming and that human activities are largely responsible has solidified in recent years.

A recent report published by the U.S. National Academy of Sciences stated that "the conclusion that the Earth system is warming and that much of this warming is very likely due to human activities" is "so thoroughly examined and tested, and supported by so many independent observations and results," that its "likelihood of subsequently being found to be wrong is vanishingly small."

The national academies of sciences of 13 leading nations issued a joint statement in 2009 stating that "climate change is happening even faster than previously estimated."

A 2009 study of the work of more than 1,300 climate researchers actively publishing in the field found that 97 to 98 percent of those researchers agree with the central theories behind global warming.

The consequences of global warming are already beginning to be experienced in the United States, and are likely to grow in the years to come, particularly if emissions of global warming pollutants continue unabated. . . .

Several types of extreme weather events have occurred more frequently or with greater intensity in recent years. Global warming may drive changes in the frequency, timing, location or severity of such events in the future.

Violent Storms and Hurricanes

The strongest tropical cyclones have been getting stronger around the globe over the last several decades, with a documented increase in the number of severe Category 4 and 5 hurricanes in the Atlantic Ocean since 1980.

Scientists project that global warming may bring fewer—but more intense—hurricanes worldwide, and that those hurricanes will bring increased precipitation. The number of intense Category 4 and 5 hurricanes in the Atlantic may nearly double over the course of the next century.

Estimated total damages from the seven most costly hurricanes to strike the United States since the beginning of 2005 exceed $200 billion. That includes damages from Hurricane Katrina, which was not only the most costly weather-related disaster of all time in the United States, but which also caused major changes to important ecosystems, including massive loss of land on barrier islands along the Gulf Coast.

Sea Level Rise and Coastal Storms

Sea level at many locations along the East Coast has been rising at a rate of nearly 1 foot per century due to the expansion of sea water as it has warmed and due to the melting of glaciers. Relative sea level has risen faster along the Gulf Coast, where land has been subsiding, and less along the northern Pacific Coast.

In addition to sea-level rise, wave heights have been rising along the northern Pacific coast in recent years, possibly indicating an increase in the intensity of Pacific winter storms. In the 1990s, scientists estimated that the height of a "100-year wave" (one expected to occur every 100 years) off the coast of the Pacific Northwest was approximately 33 feet; now it is estimated to be 46 feet.

Projected future sea-level rise of 2.5 to 6.25 feet by the end of the century would put more of the nation's coastline at risk of erosion or inundation by even today's typical coastal storms.

- In the mid-Atlantic region alone, between 900,000 and 3.4 million people live in areas that would be threatened by a 3.3 foot (1 meter) rise in sea level.
- Along the Gulf Coast from Galveston, Texas, to Mobile, Alabama, more than half the highways, nearly all the rail miles, 29 airports and almost all existing port infrastructure are at risk of flooding in the future due to higher seas and storm surges.
- Had New York City experienced a 20-inch (0.5 meter) rise in sea level over the 1997 to 2007 period (at the low end of current projections for sea level rise by the end of the century), the number of moderate coastal flooding events would have increased from zero to 136—the equivalent of a coastal flood warning every other week.

Rainfall, Floods, and Extreme Snow Storms

The number of heavy precipitation events in the United States increased by 24 percent between 1948 and 2006, with the greatest increases in New England and the Midwest. In much of the eastern part of the country, a storm so intense that once it would have been expected to occur every 50 years can now be expected to occur every 40 years.

The largest increases in heavy rainfall events in the United States are projected to occur in the Northeast and Midwest. The timing of overall precipitation is also projected to change, with increases in precipitation during the winter and spring in much of the north, but drier summers across most of the country.

Global warming is projected to bring more frequent intense precipitation events, since warmer air is capable of holding more water vapor. Changing precipitation patterns could lead to increased risk of floods.

What is now a 100-year flood in the Columbia River basin could occur once every three years by the end of the 21st century under an extreme global warming scenario, due to the combination of wetter winters and accelerated snowmelt. This change is projected to occur even as the region experiences an increase in summer drought due to reduced summer precipitation and declining availability of snowmelt in the summer.

Flooding is the most common weather-related disaster in the United States. Recent years have seen a string of incredibly destructive floods, including the 2008 Midwest flood that inundated Cedar Rapids, Iowa, and caused an estimated $8 to $10 billion in damage, and the massive 2010 floods in New England and Tennessee.

Projections of more frequent heavy precipitation apply to both rain and snow storms (although warming will bring a shift in precipitation from snow to rain over time). The 2010 record snowfalls in the mid-Atlantic region (dubbed "Snowmageddon") are fully consistent with projections of increased extreme precipitation in a warming world—and with the string of massive flooding events elsewhere in the country during 2010.

FAST FACT

According to Kevin Trenberth, senior scientist at the US National Center for Atmospheric Research, global warming has raised sea surface temperatures, which has increased the amount of water vapor in the atmosphere by about 4 percent. This extra moisture contributed to extreme rains and flooding in India, China, and Pakistan in 2010 and in Australia in 2010 and 2011.

Heat Waves, Drought, and Wildfires

Over the past century, drought has become more common in parts of the northern Rockies, the Southwest and the Southeast. Periods of extreme heat have also become more common since 1960.

Large wildfires have become more frequent in the American West since the mid-1980s, with the greatest increases in large wildfires coming in the northern Rockies and northern California.

Hurricane Rita, a category five storm, grinds its way toward the Gulf Coast in 2005. Climate change proponents say global warming is producing more category four and five hurricanes and extreme weather than in the past.

Heat waves are projected to be more frequent, more intense, and last longer in a warming world. Much of the United States—especially the Southwest—is projected to experience more frequent or more severe drought.

Scientists project that a warmer climate could lead to a 54 percent increase in the average area burned by western wildfires annually, with the greatest increases in the Pacific Northwest and Rocky Mountains.

Heat waves are among the most lethal of extreme weather events. A 2006 heat wave that affected the entire contiguous United States was blamed for at least 147 deaths in California and another 140 deaths in New York City.

Wildfire is capable of causing great damage to property, while the cost of fighting wildfires is a significant drain on public resources.

In 2008, California spent $200 million in a single month fighting a series of wildfires in the northern part of the state.

Avoiding the potential increased risks from extreme weather events—and their costs to the economy and society—is among the reasons the United States and the world should reduce emissions of global warming pollution.

EVALUATING THE AUTHOR'S ARGUMENTS:

Environment New Jersey Research & Policy Center claims that human-caused global warming is the cause of increasingly extreme weather events. What pieces of evidence does the author provide to support this claim? List at least two quotations, statistics, facts, or statements of reasoning it offers to bolster its position. Did the Environment New Jersey Research & Policy Center convince you of its argument? Explain why or why not.

Global Warming Is Not Causing Extreme Weather

Anne Jolis

"*Researchers have yet to find evidence of more-extreme weather patterns over the period [twentieth century], contrary to what the models predict.*"

In the following viewpoint Anne Jolis argues there is no evidence to show that weather is getting more extreme or that isolated extreme weather incidents have anything to do with human-caused global warming. She explains that although climate models have predicted an increase in extreme weather patterns as carbon dioxide (CO_2) levels rise, actual observed events would suggest otherwise. Jolis says that weather is by nature unpredictable and prone to many changes and cycles. For this reason, she thinks it is unwise to pour trillions of dollars into solutions that try to control climate change, especially when it is unclear they will have any effect. A smarter use of such money, she says, would be to help cities prepare for hurricanes and snowstorms so they can minimize death and destruction when extreme weather inevitably does occur.

Jolis is a reporter for the *Wall Street Journal*, where this article was originally published.

AS YOU READ, CONSIDER THE FOLLOWING QUESTIONS:
1. What is the Twentieth Century Reanalysis Project and how does it factor into the author's argument?
2. In what way did the "idea" of global warming contribute to devastating winter storms in Britain, according to the author?
3. What helped keep the death count low during Australia's Cyclone Yasi, according to Jolis?

L ast week [in February 2011] a severe storm froze Dallas under a sheet of ice, just in time to disrupt the plans of the tens of thousands of (American) football fans descending on the city for the Super Bowl. On the other side of the globe, Cyclone Yasi slammed northeastern Australia, destroying homes and crops and displacing hundreds of thousands of people.

Some climate alarmists would have us believe that these storms are yet another baleful consequence of man-made CO_2 [carbon dioxide] emissions. In addition to the latest weather events, they also point to recent cyclones in Burma, last winter's fatal chills in Nepal and Bangladesh, December's blizzards in Britain, and every other drought, typhoon and unseasonable heat wave around the world.

No Evidence of Extreme Weather Increase
But is it true? To answer that question, you need to understand whether recent weather trends are extreme by historical standards. The Twentieth Century Reanalysis Project is the latest attempt to find out, using super-computers to generate a dataset of global atmospheric circulation from 1871 to the present.

As it happens, the project's initial findings, published last month, show no evidence of an intensifying weather trend. "In the climate models, the extremes get more extreme as we move into a doubled CO_2 world in 100 years," atmospheric scientist Gilbert Compo, one of the researchers on the project, tells me from his office at the University of Colorado, Boulder. "So we were surprised that none of the three major indices of climate variability that we used show a trend of increased circulation going back to 1871."

In other words, researchers have yet to find evidence of more-extreme weather patterns over the period, contrary to what the models predict. "There's no data-driven answer yet to the question of how human activity has affected extreme weather," adds Roger Pielke Jr., another University of Colorado climate researcher.

We Still Do Not Know a Lot About Climate Change

We do know that carbon dioxide and other gases trap and re-radiate heat. We also know that humans have emitted ever-more of these gases since the Industrial Revolution. What we don't know is exactly how sensitive the climate is to increases in these gases versus other possible factors—solar variability, oceanic currents, Pacific heating and cooling cycles, planets' gravitational and magnetic oscillations, and so on.

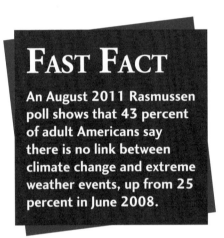

FAST FACT

An August 2011 Rasmussen poll shows that 43 percent of adult Americans say there is no link between climate change and extreme weather events, up from 25 percent in June 2008.

Given the unknowns, it's possible that even if we spend trillions of dollars, and forgo trillions more in future economic growth, to cut carbon emissions to pre-industrial levels, the climate will continue to change—as it always has.

Planning for Severe Weather Is Easy and Smart

That's not to say we're helpless. There is at least one climate lesson that we can draw from the recent weather: Whatever happens, prosperity and preparedness help. North Texas's ice storm wreaked havoc and left hundreds of football fans stranded, cold, and angry. But thanks to modern infrastructure, 21st century health care, and stockpiles of magnesium chloride and snow plows, the storm caused no reported deaths and Dallas managed to host the big game on Sunday.

Compare that outcome to the 55 people who reportedly died of pneumonia, respiratory problems and other cold-related illnesses in Bangladesh and Nepal when temperatures dropped to just above

"Weather terror," cartoon by Larry Wright, *The Detroit News,* www.CagleCartoons, February 6, 2007. Copyright © 2007 by Wright and CagleCartoons.com. All rights reserved. Reproduced by permission.

freezing last winter. Even rich countries can be caught off guard: Witness the thousands stranded when Heathrow [London's airport] skimped on de-icing supplies and let five inches of snow ground flights for two days before Christmas. Britain's GDP [gross domestic product] shrank by 0.5% in the fourth quarter of 2010, for which the Office of National Statistics mostly blames "the bad weather."

Arguably, global warming *was* a factor in that case. Or at least the idea of global warming was. The London-based Global Warming Policy Foundation charges that British authorities are so committed to the notion that Britain's future will be warmer that they have failed to plan for winter storms that have hit the country three years running.

A sliver of the billions that British taxpayers spend on trying to control their climes could have bought them more of the supplies that helped Dallas recover more quickly. And, with a fraction of *that* sliver of prosperity, more Bangladeshis and Nepalis could have acquired the antibiotics and respirators to survive their cold spell.

Weather-Related Death and Damage Can Be Prevented

A comparison of cyclones Yasi and Nargis tells a similar story: As devastating as Yasi has been, Australia's infrastructure, medicine, and emergency protocols meant the Category 5 storm has killed only one person so far. Australians are now mulling all the ways they could have better protected their property and economy.

But if they feel like counting their blessings, they need only look to the similar cyclone that hit the Irrawaddy Delta in 2008. Burma's military regime hadn't allowed for much of an economy before the cyclone, but Nargis destroyed nearly all the Delta had. Afterwards, the junta blocked foreign aid workers from delivering needed water purification and medical supplies. In the end, the government let Nargis kill more than 130,000 people.

Global-warming alarmists insist that economic activity is the problem, when the available evidence show it to be part of the solution. We may not be able to do anything about the weather, extreme or otherwise. But we can make sure we have the resources to deal with it when it comes.

EVALUATING THE AUTHOR'S ARGUMENTS:

Anne Jolis suggests that weather-related death and destruction is caused more by countries' lack of preparedness for disaster and less by extreme weather patterns brought on by global warming. What do you think the other authors in this chapter would say about this conclusion? For each author, write one or two sentences on how you think they would respond. Then, state your opinion on whether global warming is contributing to extreme weather patterns.

Chapter 3

How Can Global Warming Be Minimized?

Wind turbines are a source of renewable energy. Much controversy surrounds the financial aspects of renewable energy.

Reducing Air Pollution Can Slow Global Warming

"Reducing soot and the other short-lived pollutants would not stop global warming, but it would buy time . . . for the world to put in place more costly efforts to regulate carbon dioxide."

Veerabhadran Ramanathan and David G. Victor

In the following viewpoint Veerabhadran Ramanathan and David G. Victor argue that global warming can be slowed by reducing air pollution. They acknowledge that global warming solutions that involve reducing carbon dioxide (CO_2) emissions are expensive, take decades, and are unpopular because they require people to drastically change their lifestyles. But CO_2 is not the only greenhouse gas that contributes to global warming, they say. Other compounds, especially those found in air pollution, also contribute to global warming. Instituting simple, easy, and relatively inexpensive antipollution measures could reduce many of these gases, which include methane, ozone, and soot. They conclude that cutting air pollution could buy society much-needed time as more long-term solutions to global warming are worked out.

Ramanathan is the director of the Center for Atmospheric Sciences at the Scripps Institution of Oceanography at the University of California, San Diego, where David G. Victor is a professor at the School of International Relations and Pacific Studies.

AS YOU READ, CONSIDER THE FOLLOWING QUESTIONS:
1. What is a hydrofluorocarbon, as described by the authors?
2. What effect do the authors say substituting less polluting substances for hydrofluorocarbons could have on global warming?
3. How many deaths does soot cause each year, according to Ramanathan and Victor?

As the curtain rises tomorrow [November 28, 2010] in Cancún, Mexico, on the next round of international talks on climate change, expectations are low that the delegates will agree on a new treaty to reduce emissions that contribute to global warming. They were unable to do so last year [at climate-related talks] in Copenhagen, and since then the negotiating positions of the biggest countries have grown even further apart.

Yet it is still possible to make significant progress. To give these talks their best chance for success, the delegates in Cancún should move beyond their focus on long-term efforts to stop warming and take a few immediate, practical actions that could have a tangible effect on the climate in the coming decades.

Carbon Dioxide Is Just One of the Problems

The opportunity to make progress arises from the fact that global warming is caused by two separate types of pollution. One is the long-term buildup of carbon dioxide, which can remain in the atmosphere for centuries. Diplomacy has understandably focused on this problem because, without deep cuts in carbon dioxide emissions, there can be no permanent solution to warming.

The carbon dioxide problem is hard to fix, however, because it comes mainly from the burning of fossil fuels, which is so essential to modern life and commerce. It will take decades and trillions of dollars to convert all the world's fossil-fuel-based energy systems to cleaner systems like nuclear, solar and wind power. In the meantime, a fast-action plan is needed.

Other Kinds of Pollution Contribute to Warming

But carbon dioxide is not the only kind of pollution that contributes to global warming. Other potent warming agents include three short-lived gases—methane, some hydrofluorocarbons and lower atmospheric ozone—and dark soot particles. The warming effect of these pollutants, which stay in the atmosphere for several days to about a decade, is already about 80 percent of the amount that carbon dioxide causes. The world could easily and quickly reduce these pollutants; the technology and regulatory systems needed to do so are already in place.

Take methane, for example, which is 25 times more powerful than carbon dioxide in causing warming. It is emitted by coal mines, landfills, rice paddies and livestock. And because it is the main ingredient in natural gas, it leaks from many older natural-gas pipelines. With relatively minor changes—for example, replacing old gas pipelines, better managing the water used in rice cultivation (so that less of the rice rots) and collecting the methane emitted by landfills—it would be possible to lower methane emissions by 40 percent. Since saved methane is a valuable fuel, some of this effort could pay for itself.

Unfortunately, the accounting systems used in climate diplomacy are cumbersome and offer relatively few incentives for countries to make much effort to control methane.

> **FAST FACT**
>
> The Union of Concerned Scientists reports that pollution particles between 0.1 and 1 micron in size with a high amount of black carbon—that is, soot, produced by burning of fossil fuels and biofuels—absorb sunlight, heating the atmosphere and accelerating melting when particles land on snow and ice. Therefore, efforts to reduce black pollution, such as by distributing low-soot cookstoves in developing countries, could curb global warming.

Envoys from 190 countries met in Cancún in November 2010 to try to produce a new treaty to reduce emissions that contribute to global warming. The countries that produce the most emissions have grown further apart in their negotiating positions and no compromise could be reached.

Modest Cuts Could Have a Big Effect

Big cuts are also possible in hydrofluorocarbons, or HFCs, many of which are used as refrigerants in air-conditioners and other cooling systems. The most troubling of the short-lived HFCs were invented to replace chlorofluorocarbons, refrigerants that were thinning the ozone layer in the upper atmosphere, and were also a major warming agent. Chlorofluorocarbons were regulated under the Montreal Protocol starting in 1987.

The warming effect of these HFCs is at least 1,000 times that of carbon dioxide. Unless they are regulated as chlorofluorocarbons have been, their warming effect will increase substantially in the coming decades.

Shifting from HFCs to substitutes that are 100 times less potent as climate warmers could offset nearly a decade's increase in warming that is expected from rising emissions of carbon dioxide. The delegates in Cancún would need only to ask that the Montreal Protocol take on the further authority to regulate HFCs.

Cleaning the Air Would Have Multiple Benefits

From a political point of view, the most appealing greenhouse emissions to reduce are ozone and soot, because they contribute so much to local air pollution. After all, people everywhere care about the quality of the air they breathe and see—even if most of them are not yet very worried about global warming. A desire to clean up the air is a rare point of commonality between developing and industrialized nations.

Ozone, which is formed in the lower atmosphere from carbon monoxide, methane and other gases emitted by human activity, is a particularly hazardous component of urban smog. And every year it causes tens of billions of dollars in damage to crops worldwide. So pollution restrictions that reduce ozone levels, especially in the rapidly growing polluted cities of Asia, could both clear the air and slow warming.

Soot likewise offers an opportunity to marry local interests with the global good. A leading cause of respiratory diseases, soot is responsible for some 1.9 million deaths a year. It also melts ice and snow packs. Thus, sooty emissions from Asia, Europe and North America are helping to thin the Arctic ice. And soot from India, China and a few other countries threatens water supplies fed by the Himalayan-Tibetan glaciers.

New air pollution regulations could help reduce soot. Such laws in California have cut diesel-soot emissions in that state by half. In China and India, a program to improve power generation, filter soot from diesel engines, reduce emissions from brick-making kilns and provide more efficient cookstoves could cut the levels of soot in those regions by about two-thirds—and benefit countries downwind as well.

Cutting Pollution Could Buy Us Much-Needed Time

Reducing soot and the other short-lived pollutants would not stop global warming, but it would buy time, perhaps a few decades, for the world to put in place more costly efforts to regulate carbon dioxide. And it would help the major economies demonstrate credibility on climate change, which has been in short supply in the diplomatic talks so far.

The impasse that was evident in Copenhagen last year and is likely to reappear in Cancún arises in part from the inability of China, India, Europe and the United States to show that they are adopting practical measures to slow climate change. Agreeing on a shared strategy to curtail short-lived pollutants would be a good way for all of them to start.

Global Warming Solutions Can Be Simple

Credibility is especially important for the United States. It can already offer the world much of the technology and regulatory expertise that will be needed to reduce short-lived pollutants, particularly ozone and soot. Some American efforts are under way to share these technologies, including a program to help provide better cookstoves for people in developing countries. By making such programs more visible and demonstrating that they deliver tangible results, and by establishing a realistic plan for cutting its own emissions at home, the United States could show that it is serious about addressing climate change.

For too long, overly ambitious global climate talks have focused on the aspects of global warming that are hardest to solve. A few more modest steps, with quick and measurable effects, are a better way to proceed.

EVALUATING THE AUTHORS' ARGUMENTS:

Veerabhadran Ramanathan and David G. Victor use facts, statistics, examples, and reasoning to make their argument that reducing air pollution can slow global warming. They do not, however, use any quotations to support their point. If you were to rewrite this article and insert quotations, what authorities might you quote? Where would you place them, and why?

Reducing Some Air Pollutants Will Accelerate Global Warming

"The world is running short on air pollution, and if we continue to cut back on smoke pouring forth from industrial smokestacks, the increase in global warming could be profound."

Eli Kintisch

In the following viewpoint Eli Kintisch explains that cleaner air might actually speed global warming. He discusses how sulfate particles and aerosols—caused from burning coal—actually help keep the planet cool. Much like particles and debris spewed from a volcano, Kintisch explains that these air pollutants block out the sun and prevent the planet from warming, even as carbon dioxide (CO_2) emissions rise. He explains that temperatures have risen as such pollutants have been cleared from the air. Kintisch argues it is noble to want cleaner air, but too much of a good thing could be counterproductive in the fight to slow global warming. He concludes that ultimately there are no shortcuts for reducing global warming—cutting CO_2 emissions must be part of any solution.

Kintisch is the author of *Hack the Planet: Science's Best Hope—or Worst Nightmare—for Averting Climate Catastrophe.*

AS YOU READ, CONSIDER THE FOLLOWING QUESTIONS:
1. By what percent does Kintisch say sulfate aerosols have been reduced since the 1980s?
2. How long do aerosols last in the air, according to Kintisch?
3. What does Kintisch say happened after China took measures to cut sulfate pollution?

You're likely to hear a chorus of dire warnings as we approach Earth Day [in April 2010], but there's a serious shortage few pundits are talking about: air pollution. That's right, the world is running short on air pollution, and if we continue to cut back on smoke pouring forth from industrial smokestacks, the increase in global warming could be profound.

Cleaner Air Is a Double-Edged Sword

Cleaner air, one of the signature achievements of the U.S. environmental movement, is certainly worth celebrating. Scientists estimate that the U.S. Clean Air Act has cut a major air pollutant called sulfate aerosols, for example, by 30% to 50% since the 1980s, helping greatly reduce cases of asthma and other respiratory problems.

But even as industrialized and developing nations alike steadily reduce aerosol pollution—caused primarily by burning coal—climate scientists are beginning to understand just how much these tiny particles have helped keep the planet cool. A silent benefit of sulfates, in fact, is that they've been helpfully blocking sunlight from striking the Earth for many decades, by brightening clouds and expanding their coverage. Emerging science suggests that their underappreciated impact has been incredible.

Sulfates and Aerosols Help Keep Earth Cool

Researchers believe greenhouse gases such as CO_2 [carbon dioxide] have committed the Earth to an eventual warming of roughly 4 degrees Fahrenheit, a quarter of which the planet has already experienced. Thanks to cooling by aerosols starting in the 1940s, however, the planet has only felt a portion of that greenhouse warming. In the 1980s, sulfate pollution dropped as Western nations enhanced pollution controls, and as a result, global warming accelerated.

There's hot debate over the size of what amounts to a cooling mask, but there's no question that it will diminish as industries continue to clean traditional pollutants from their smokestacks. Unlike CO_2, which persists in the atmosphere for centuries, aerosols last for a week at most in the air. So cutting them would probably accelerate global warming rapidly.

In a recent paper in the journal *Climate Dynamics*, modelers forecast what would happen if nations instituted all existing pollution controls on industrial sources and vehicles by 2030. They found the current rate of warming—roughly 0.4 degrees Fahrenheit per decade—doubled worldwide, and nearly tripled in North America.

Despite intransigence on carbon emissions, even China is taking aggressive steps to cut sulfate pollution, and temperatures have risen as a result.

> ## FAST FACT
>
> Some pollution particles— namely low-carbon "white" pollution such as sulfate particles—reflect solar radiation, temporarily making the earth a bit cooler than it would be if white pollution were reduced. The US Geological Survey calculates, for example, that sulfate emissions from the 1991 Pinatubo volcanic eruption cooled the earth's surface by 0.6°C (1°F) for one to two years.

We Must Pick and Choose Our Pollutants

But surely the answer can't be to slow our drive to clean our air. One way to buy time might be to tackle another air pollutant that warms the planet: soot. In 2008, scientists estimated that so-called black carbon, soot's prime component, is responsible for 60% more global warming above that caused by greenhouse gases. Cleaner-burning diesel engines in the West and more efficient cookstoves in the developing world are the answer. But on both scores, "relatively little has been done to address the problem," says the Boston-based Clean Air Task Force.

When coal is burned it introduces sulphates and aerosols into the atmosphere. Some claim the production of aerosols and sulphates helps keep the planet cool.

In the face of severe climate risks, credible scientists are beginning to study geo-engineering—tinkering with global systems to reduce warming directly. One scheme is to spew sulfates or other sun-blocking particles miles high in the stratosphere. If it worked, it would mimic the natural cooling effect of volcanoes, replacing the near-surface sulfate mask with a much higher one. But the possible side effects could be dire, including damage to the ozone layer. The potential geopolitical implications, like wars over the thermostat, could be devastating as well.

We might need geo-engineering to stave off the worst effects of the warming. But most climate scientists think we're not there yet. And so the most important thing we can do now is to train our sights on both the unexpectedly helpful sulfates and the unexpectedly pernicious carbon. We can't continue to only focus on traditional pollutants without reducing greenhouse emissions. We simply have to find a way to clean our air of both.

EVALUATING THE AUTHOR'S ARGUMENTS:

In this viewpoint Eli Kintisch argues that aerosol pollution—caused primarily by burning coal—helps keep the earth cool. But in the previous viewpoint, Veerabhadran Ramanathan and David G. Victor argue that methane pollution—a different byproduct of the coal industry—causes warming. How might you make sense of this contradiction? Ultimately, do you think the coal industry contributes to global warming, or not? Explain your reasoning and quote from the text that made most sense to you.

A Plan to Power 100 Percent of the Planet with Renewables

"A large-scale wind, water and solar energy system can reliably supply the world's needs, significantly benefiting climate, air quality, water quality, ecology and energy security."

Mark Z. Jacobson and Mark A. Delucchi

In the following viewpoint Mark Z. Jacobson and Mark A. Delucchi lay out a plan for powering the world entirely on renewable sources of energy, which they say is the best way to prevent global warming. Jacobson and Delucchi say there is enough wind, water, and solar energy to power every single aspect of modern human life, from electricity to cars to airplanes to cooking stoves. They calculate that renewable energy can be as cheap as fossil fuel energy and predict renewable power plants will take up even less space than current coal plants. They explain how power can be generated from renewables even when the sun is not shining or the wind not blowing. Jacobson and Delucchi admit there are obstacles to transitioning to a renewable energy system, but believe all of these can

Mark Z. Jacobson and Mark A. Delucchi, "A Plan to Power 100 Percent of the Planet with Renewables," *Scientific American,* October 26, 2009. Copyright © 2009 by Scientific American, a division of Nature America, Inc.

be overcome. They conclude that transitioning to a renewable energy system is the best chance for preventing global warming and for solving other environmental and health problems caused by fossil fuel use.

Jacobson is a civil and environmental engineering professor at Stanford University. Delucchi is a research scientist at the Institute of Transportation Studies at University of California, Davis.

AS YOU READ, CONSIDER THE FOLLOWING QUESTIONS:
1. How much more efficient is it to use electricity than gasoline, according to the authors?
2. What percent of the earth's land would the wind turbines needed for Jacobson and Delucchi's plan take up?
3. For how much of the year do Jacobson and Delucchi say the average coal plant is offline? What about the average wind turbine?

I n December leaders from around the world will meet in Copenhagen to try to agree on cutting back greenhouse gas emissions for decades to come. The most effective step to implement that goal would be a massive shift away from fossil fuels to clean, renewable energy sources. If leaders can have confidence that such a transformation is possible, they might commit to an historic agreement. We think they can.

A year ago former vice president Al Gore threw down a gauntlet: to repower America with 100 percent carbon-free electricity within 10 years. As the two of us started to evaluate the feasibility of such a change, we took on an even larger challenge: to determine how 100 percent of the world's energy, for *all* purposes, could be supplied by wind, water and solar resources, by as early as 2030. Our plan is presented here.

Scientists have been building to this moment for at least a decade, analyzing various pieces of the challenge. Most recently, a 2009 Stanford University study ranked energy systems according to their impacts on global warming, pollution, water supply, land use, wildlife and other concerns. The very best options were wind, solar, geothermal, tidal and hydroelectric power—all of which are driven by wind, water or sunlight (referred to as WWS). Nuclear power, coal with carbon capture, and ethanol were all poorer options, as were oil and natural gas. The study also found that battery-electric vehicles and hydrogen fuel-cell vehicles recharged by WWS options would largely eliminate pollution from the transportation sector.

Our plan calls for millions of wind turbines, water machines and solar installations. The numbers are large, but the scale is not an insurmountable hurdle; society has achieved massive transformations before. During World War II, the U.S. retooled automobile factories to produce 300,000 aircraft, and other countries produced 486,000 more. In 1956 the U.S. began building the Interstate Highway System, which after 35 years extended for 47,000 miles, changing commerce and society.

Is it feasible to transform the world's energy systems? Could it be accomplished in two decades? The answers depend on the technologies chosen, the availability of critical materials, and economic and political factors.

Clean Technologies Only

Renewable energy comes from enticing sources: wind, which also produces waves; water, which includes hydroelectric, tidal and geothermal energy (water heated by hot underground rock); and sun, which includes photovoltaics and solar power plants that focus sunlight to heat a fluid that drives a turbine to generate electricity. Our plan includes only technologies that work or are close to working today on a large scale, rather than those that may exist 20 or 30 years from now.

To ensure that our system remains clean, we consider only technologies that have near-zero emissions of greenhouse gases and air pollutants over their entire life cycle, including construction, operation and decommissioning. For example, when burned in vehicles, even the most ecologically acceptable sources of ethanol create air pollution that will cause the same mortality level as when gasoline is burned. Nuclear power results in up to 25 times more carbon emissions than wind energy, when reactor construction and uranium refining and transport are considered. Carbon capture and sequestration technology can reduce carbon dioxide emissions from coal-fired power plants but will increase air pollutants and will extend all the other deleterious effects of coal mining, transport and processing, because more coal must be burned to power the capture and storage steps. Similarly, we consider only technologies that do not present significant waste disposal or terrorism risks.

In our plan, WWS will supply electric power for heating and transportation—industries that will have to revamp if the world has any hope of slowing climate change. We have assumed that most fossil-fuel heating (as well as ovens and stoves) can be replaced by electric systems and that most fossil-fuel transportation can be replaced by battery and fuel-cell vehicles. Hydrogen, produced by using WWS electricity to split water (electrolysis), would power fuel cells and be burned in airplanes and by industry.

Plenty of Supply

Today the maximum power consumed worldwide at any given moment is about 12.5 trillion watts (terawatts, or TW), according to the U.S. Energy Information Administration. The agency projects that in 2030 the world will require 16.9 TW of power as global population and living standards rise, with about 2.8 TW in the U.S. The mix of sources is similar to today's, heavily dependent on fossil fuels. If, however, the planet were powered entirely by WWS, with no fossil-fuel or biomass combustion, an intriguing savings would occur. Global power demand would be only 11.5 TW, and U.S. demand would be 1.8 TW. That decline occurs because, in most cases, electrification is a more efficient way to use energy. For example, only 17 to 20 percent of the energy in gasoline is used to move a vehicle (the rest is wasted as heat), whereas 75 to 86 percent of the electricity delivered to an electric vehicle goes into motion.

Even if demand did rise to 16.9 TW, WWS sources could provide far more power. Detailed studies by us and others indicate that energy from the wind, worldwide, is about 1,700 TW. Solar, alone, offers 6,500 TW. Of course, wind and sun out in the open seas, over high mountains and across protected regions would not be available. If we subtract these and low-wind areas not likely to be developed, we are still left with 40 to 85 TW for wind and 580 TW for solar, each far beyond future human demand. Yet currently we generate only 0.02

TW of wind power and 0.008 TW of solar. These sources hold an incredible amount of untapped potential.

The other WWS technologies will help create a flexible range of options. Although all the sources can expand greatly, for practical reasons, wave power can be extracted only near coastal areas. Many geothermal sources are too deep to be tapped economically. And even though hydroelectric power now exceeds all other WWS sources, most of the suitable large reservoirs are already in use.

The Plan: Power Plants Required

Clearly, enough renewable energy exists. How, then, would we transition to a new infrastructure to provide the world with 11.5 TW? We have chosen a mix of technologies emphasizing wind and solar, with about 9 percent of demand met by mature water-related methods. (Other combinations of wind and solar could be as successful.)

Wind supplies 51 percent of the demand, provided by 3.8 million large wind turbines (each rated at five megawatts) worldwide. Although that quantity may sound enormous, it is interesting to note

In Jacobson and Delucchi's plan, 3.8 million wind turbines would supply 51 percent of the total demand for power. Water power and solar sources would provide for the remainder of the demand.

that the world manufactures 73 million cars and light trucks *every year*. Another 40 percent of the power comes from photovoltaics and concentrated solar plants, with about 30 percent of the photovoltaic output from rooftop panels on homes and commercial buildings. About 89,000 photovoltaic and concentrated solar power plants, averaging 300 megawatts apiece, would be needed. Our mix also includes 900 hydroelectric stations worldwide, 70 percent of which are already in place.

Only about 0.8 percent of the wind base is installed today. The worldwide footprint of the 3.8 million turbines would be less than 50 square kilometers (smaller than Manhattan). When the needed spacing between them is figured, they would occupy about 1 percent of the earth's land, but the empty space among turbines could be used for agriculture or ranching or as open land or ocean. The nonrooftop photovoltaics and concentrated solar plants would occupy about 0.33 percent of the planet's land. Building such an extensive infrastructure will take time. But so did the current power plant network. And remember that if we stick with fossil fuels, demand by 2030 will rise to 16.9 TW, requiring about 13,000 large new coal plants, which themselves would occupy a lot more land, as would the mining to supply them.

The Materials Hurdle

The scale of the WWS infrastructure is not a barrier. But a few materials needed to build it could be scarce or subject to price manipulation.

Enough concrete and steel exist for the millions of wind turbines, and both those commodities are fully recyclable. The most problematic materials may be rare-earth metals such as neodymium used in turbine gearboxes. Although the metals are not in short supply, the low-cost sources are concentrated in China, so countries such as the U.S. could be trading dependence on Middle Eastern oil for dependence on Far Eastern metals. Manufacturers are moving toward gearless turbines, however, so that limitation may become moot.

Photovoltaic cells rely on amorphous or crystalline silicon, cadmium telluride, or copper indium selenide and sulfide. Limited supplies of tellurium and indium could reduce the prospects for some types of thin-film solar cells, though not for all; the other types might be able to take up the slack. Large-scale production could be restricted by the silver that cells require, but finding ways to reduce the silver content could tackle that hurdle. Recycling parts from old cells could ameliorate material difficulties as well.

Three components could pose challenges for building millions of electric vehicles: rare-earth metals for electric motors, lithium for lithium-ion batteries and platinum for fuel cells. More than half the world's lithium reserves lie in Bolivia and Chile. That concentration, combined with rapidly growing demand, could raise prices significantly. More problematic is the claim by Meridian International Research that not enough economically recoverable lithium exists to build anywhere near the number of batteries needed in a global electric-vehicle economy. Recycling could change the equation, but the economics of recycling depend in part on whether batteries are made with easy recyclability in mind, an issue the industry is aware of. The long-term use of platinum also depends on recycling; current available reserves would sustain annual production of 20 million fuel-cell vehicles, along with existing industrial uses, for fewer than 100 years.

Smart Mix for Reliability

A new infrastructure must provide energy on demand at least as reliably as the existing infrastructure. WWS technologies generally suffer less downtime than traditional sources. The average U.S. coal plant is offline 12.5 percent of the year for scheduled and unscheduled maintenance. Modern wind turbines have a down time of less than 2 percent on land and less than 5 percent at sea. Photovoltaic systems are also at less than 2 percent. Moreover, when an individual wind, solar or wave device is down, only a small fraction of production is affected; when a coal, nuclear or natural gas plant goes offline, a large chunk of generation is lost.

The main WWS challenge is that the wind does not always blow and the sun does not always shine in a given location. Intermittency problems can be mitigated by a smart balance of sources, such as generating a base supply from steady geothermal or tidal power, relying on wind at night when it is often plentiful, using solar by day and turning to a reliable source such as hydroelectric that can be turned on and off quickly to smooth out supply or meet peak demand. For example, interconnecting wind farms that are only 100 to 200 miles apart can compensate for hours of zero power at any one farm should the wind not be blowing there. Also helpful is interconnecting geographically dispersed sources so they can back up one another, installing smart electric meters in homes that automatically recharge electric vehicles when demand is low and building facilities that store power for later use.

Because the wind often blows during stormy conditions when the sun does not shine and the sun often shines on calm days with little wind, combining wind and solar can go a long way toward meeting demand, especially when geothermal provides a steady base and hydroelectric can be called on to fill in the gaps.

As Cheap as Coal

The mix of WWS sources in our plan can reliably supply the residential, commercial, industrial and transportation sectors. The logical next question is whether the power would be affordable. For each technology, we calculated how much it would cost a producer to generate power and transmit it across the grid. We included the annualized cost of capital, land, operations, maintenance, energy storage to help offset intermittent supply, and transmission. Today the cost of wind, geothermal and hydroelectric are all less than seven cents a kilowatt-hour ($\cent$/kWh); wave and solar are higher. But by 2020 and beyond wind, wave and hydro are expected to be 4$\cent$/kWh or less.

For comparison, the average cost in the U.S. in 2007 of conventional power generation and transmission was about 7$\cent$/kWh, and it

> # FAST FACT
>
> The US Energy Information Administration reports the average annual electricity consumption of a US household in 2009 was 10,896 kilowatt-hours (kWh). To supply that much electricity, power plants emit an estimated 6.46 metric tons (7.12 tons) of CO_2. In contrast, a residential solar energy system emits no CO_2, a per-household reduction of 161.5 metric tons (178 tons) of atmospheric CO_2 over the estimated twenty-five-year life of a solar photovoltaic (PV) system.

is projected to be 8¢/kWh in 2020. Power from wind turbines, for example, already costs about the same or less than it does from a new coal or natural gas plant, and in the future wind power is expected to be the least costly of all options. The competitive cost of wind has made it the second-largest source of new electric power generation in the U.S. for the past three years, behind natural gas and ahead of coal.

Solar power is relatively expensive now but should be competitive as early as 2020. A careful analysis by Vasilis Fthenakis of Brookhaven National Laboratory indicates that within 10 years, photovoltaic system costs could drop to about 10¢/kWh, including long-distance transmission and the cost of compressed-air storage of power for use at night. The same analysis estimates that concentrated solar power systems with enough thermal storage to generate electricity 24 hours a day in spring, summer and fall could deliver electricity at 10¢/kWh or less.

Transportation in a WWS world will be driven by batteries or fuel cells, so we should compare the economics of these electric vehicles with that of internal-combustion-engine vehicles. Detailed analyses by one of us (Delucchi) and Tim Lipman of the University of California, Berkeley, have indicated that mass-produced electric vehicles with advanced lithium-ion or nickel metal-hydride batteries could have a full lifetime cost per mile (including battery replacements) that is comparable with that of a gasoline vehicle, when gasoline sells for more than $2 a gallon.

When the so-called externality costs (the monetary value of damages to human health, the environment and climate) of fossil-fuel generation are taken into account, WWS technologies become even more cost-competitive.

Overall construction cost for a WWS system might be on the order of $100 trillion worldwide, over 20 years, not including transmission. But this is not money handed out by governments or consumers. It is investment that is paid back through the sale of electricity and energy. And again, relying on traditional sources would raise output from 12.5 to 16.9 TW, requiring thousands more of those plants, costing roughly $10 trillion, not to mention tens of trillions of dollars more in health, environmental and security costs. The WWS plan gives the world a new, clean, efficient energy system rather than an old, dirty, inefficient one.

Political Will

Our analyses strongly suggest that the costs of WWS will become competitive with traditional sources. In the interim, however, certain forms of WWS power will be significantly more costly than fossil power. Some combination of WWS subsidies and carbon taxes would thus be needed for a time. A feed-in tariff (FIT) program to cover the difference between generation cost and wholesale electricity prices is especially effective at scaling-up new technologies. Combining FITs with a so-called declining clock auction, in which the right to sell power to the grid goes to the lowest bidders, provides continuing incentive for WWS developers to lower costs. As that happens, FITs can be phased out. FITs have been implemented in a number of European countries and a few U.S. states and have been quite successful in stimulating solar power in Germany.

Taxing fossil fuels or their use to reflect their environmental damages also makes sense. But at a minimum, existing subsidies for fossil energy,

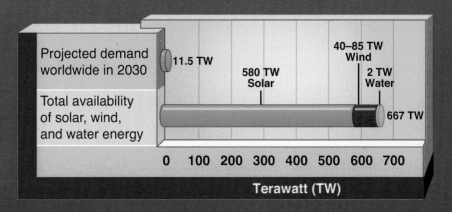

An Abundance of Renewable Energy

Jacobson and Delucchi argue that since the sun shines, the wind blows, and water flows around the world daily, eliminating wind and sun resources in inaccessible areas (i.e., open seas, high mountains, and protected regions) still leaves an incredible amount of untapped potential renewable energy sources.

Projected demand worldwide in 2030 — 11.5 TW

Total availability of solar, wind, and water energy

40–85 TW Wind
580 TW Solar
2 TW Water
667 TW

0 100 200 300 400 500 600 700

Terawatt (TW)

Taken from: Mark Z. Jacobson and Mark A. Delucchi. "A Plan to Power 100 Percent of the Planet with Renewables." *Scientific American*, October 26, 2009.

such as tax benefits for exploration and extraction, should be eliminated to level the playing field. Misguided promotion of alternatives that are less desirable than WWS power, such as farm and production subsidies for biofuels, should also be ended, because it delays deployment of cleaner systems. For their part, legislators crafting policy must find ways to resist lobbying by the entrenched energy industries.

Finally, each nation needs to be willing to invest in a robust, long-distance transmission system that can carry large quantities of WWS power from remote regions where it is often greatest—such as the Great Plains for wind and the desert Southwest for solar in the U.S.—to centers of consumption, typically cities. Reducing consumer demand during peak usage periods also requires a smart grid that gives generators and consumers much more control over electricity usage hour by hour.

A large-scale wind, water and solar energy system can reliably supply the world's needs, significantly benefiting climate, air quality, water quality, ecology and energy security. As we have shown, the obstacles are primarily political, not technical. A combination of feed-in tariffs plus incentives for providers to reduce costs, elimination of fossil subsidies and an intelligently expanded grid could be enough to ensure rapid deployment. Of course, changes in the real-world power and transportation industries will have to overcome sunk investments in existing infrastructure. But with sensible policies, nations could set a goal of generating 25 percent of their new energy supply with WWS sources in 10 to 15 years and almost 100 percent of new supply in 20 to 30 years. With extremely aggressive policies, all existing fossil-fuel capacity could theoretically be retired and replaced in the same period, but with more modest and likely policies full replacement may take 40 to 50 years. Either way, clear leadership is needed, or else nations will keep trying technologies promoted by industries rather than vetted by scientists.

A decade ago it was not clear that a global WWS system would be technically or economically feasible. Having shown that it is, we hope global leaders can figure out how to make WWS power politically feasible as well. They can start by committing to meaningful climate and renewable energy goals now.

Note: This article was originally printed with the title, "A Path to Sustainable Energy by 2030."

EVALUATING THE AUTHORS' ARGUMENTS:

Mark Z. Jacobson and Mark A. Delucchi acknowledge that their plan to transition to an entirely renewable energy system would be a very aggressive undertaking. But they remind readers that Americans have succeeded at similarly large-scale, seemingly impossible infrastructure transformations in the past, specifically after World War II. What do you think? Is it reasonable to compare post–World War II infrastructure development to transitioning to a renewable system of power to avert global warming? Why or why not? Explain your reasoning and cite examples from the text.

Switching to Renewable Energy Is Prohibitively Expensive

"Perhaps the best way to look at running the world exclusively on renewable power is that it would cost $33,500 for every man, woman and child on Earth."

Doug L. Hoffman

In the following viewpoint Doug L. Hoffman argues that switching to renewable energy is impossible because it is too expensive. He explains that people who propose a transition to a renewable energy system do not take into account the full cost of such a transition. According to his calculations, it would cost hundreds of trillions of dollars to build the required power plants, install them, upgrade power grids, and invent new machines and vehicles that could run on renewable power. A much cheaper and more reasonable plan for combating global warming is to increase reliance on nuclear power, which Hoffman says is cheap, safe, and reliable. He concludes that proposing to fight global warming by switching entirely to renewable energy will bankrupt the world and should not be attempted.

Hoffman has worked as a mathematician, an engineer, and as a college professor. He cohosts *The Resilient Earth*, a blog that provides skeptical commentary about global warming and other science issues.

AS YOU READ, CONSIDER THE FOLLOWING QUESTIONS:
1. How much does Hoffman say the total bill would be to transition to a wind, water, and solar energy system?
2. What other challenges, in addition to cost, does Hoffman say come with transitioning to an entirely renewable system? Name at least two.
3. What is Hoffman's concern about underdeveloped economies contributing to costs of the transition to renewable power?

G reen advocates and climate change alarmists alike insist that the world shift to using only non-polluting, renewable energy sources, and the sooner the better. What is seldom mentioned is the enormous cost of retooling the world's energy infrastructure to use intermittent, unreliable wind and solar energy. A recent two part paper [by Mark Z. Jacobson and Mark A. Delucchi], appearing in *Energy Policy*, makes a reasonable attempt at stating the requirements to fix humanity's fossil fuel addiction and go all green. The analysis found that, to provide roughly 84% of the world's energy needs in 2030, would require around 4 million 5 MW [megawatt] wind turbines and 90,000 300 MW solar power plants, with the remaining 16% coming from solar photovoltaic rooftop systems, geothermal, tidal, wave and hydroelectric sources. Some quick back-of-the-envelope calculations show why the world economy cannot afford to go totally green.

It Would Cost Trillions to Switch to a Renewable System

Most of the financial figures given tor renewable energy are carefully chosen to show green energy in a positive light. The facts are renewable energy is still much more expensive than conventional electrical generation. And to be accurate, government subsidies and grants cannot be used to discount the cost because, in the end, it is the total cost to society that counts. Whether a power company, the government or consumers pay it all costs the economy. Looking at generation costs without considering initial purchase, installation and integration costs are also misleading. Quite frankly, there is no way the cost of WWS [wind, water, and solar energy] would be similar to energy cost today based on initial purchase cost alone. . . .

There is enough detail in these papers to put even the most enthusiastic energy policy wonk to sleep. That is why here, as in other articles referring to these findings, the requirements have been simplified to 4 million 5 MW wind turbines and 90,000 300 MW solar power plants, ignoring the remaining 16% coming from rooftop solar panels, geothermal, tidal, wave and other sources. Using just the two primary sources, wind and solar, some quick calculations put the enormity of any replacement program into perspective:

The cost of large commercial wind turbines varies from $1 to $2 million per MW of nameplate capacity. Turbines 2 MW in size cost roughly $2.8 million installed. Ballpark figures for a 5 MW wind farm would expect to cost in the region of $9.7–14 (€7–10) million, whether from a signal large turbine or a constellation of smaller units. The figure represents the total project cost and includes the feasibility studies, EIS [environmental impact statement] and planning application, civil and electrical engineering works, grid connection costs. Let's call it $10 million per 5 MW installed. Calculating the total cost for world wind power:

4,000,000 * $10,000,000 = $40 Trillion

The solar component calls for the use of industrial scale concentrating solar plants, the most cost efficient form of solar power. Abengoa Solar, a company currently constructing solar thermal plants, put the cost of a 300 MW plant at 1.2 billion euros in 2007. In 2009, the Arizona state government announced a 200 MW plant for 1 billion

A Comparison of Costs for Various Electricity Production Methods

A 2010 analysis of various energy sources that considered construction, production, and other costs found solar energy to be far more expensive than other energy sources. Cost is but one of the reasons opponents argue it is unrealistic to power the world on renewable energy alone.

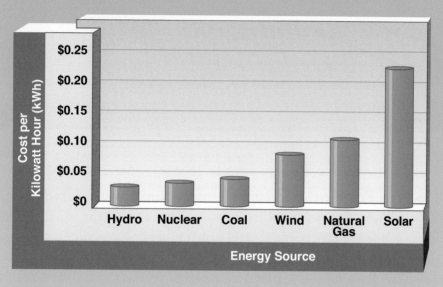

Taken from: Jason Morgan. "Comparing Energy Costs of Nuclear, Coal, Gas, Wind and Solar." NuclearFissionary.com, April 2, 2010.

US dollars so let's split the difference and estimate $1.56 billion per plant. Calculating the total cost for world solar power:

90,000 * $1,560,000,000 = $140 Trillion

So, for 84% of the needed capacity the initial purchase and installation cost is 12 times the total yearly GDP [gross domestic product] of the USA. For comparison, using a power factor of 35%, the wind plants could be replaced by 1,000 nuclear plants at $12 billion apiece (2 GW [gigawatts] each), totaling $12 trillion. The solar plants would require 4500 nuclear plants to replace them. This would cost $54 trillion. Renewable is 270% more than nuclear. And this is using a nuclear critic approved cost of $12 million per plant.

Some alternative energies like solar power are more expensive than fossil fuels, and thus some regard them as an unrealistic energy source.

Do Not Forget the Cost of Upgrading Power Grids

Current manufacturers of nuclear power plants outside the US are quoting much lower cost per unit (and much faster construction times, but that's another matter). Westinghouse claims that its AP1000 will cost $1 billion for a 1.15 GW plant. That would reduce the above estimates by a factor of 6. In other words, total nuclear cost would be $9 trillion, making the renewable "solution" 2000% (20x) more expensive.

It should also be noted that the above costs are without the necessary, continent spanning power grids needed to match spotty wind and solar power with demand. It has been estimated that to upgrade the US power grid to accommodate renewable energy sources will cost $2 trillion over the next 20 years. While a system using nuclear power will undoubtedly need to be expanded in the future, because nuclear is baseload power (i.e. steady), it would not require the extra expense of intermittent sources such as wind, solar or wave. If we use total population as an indication of demand, and hence grid infrastructure need, this adds another $45 trillion to the WWS requirements.

It Would Cost the World Every Cent It Has

The total bill for WWS comes to around $225 trillion over the next 20 years. That is nearly the entire output of the world's largest economy every year for two decades. Greens will say that once the system has been converted the energy costs drop, after all wind and sunshine are free. True, but fuel costs for nuclear power are also very low, and $150 Trillion will buy a lot of uranium and thorium. And we know nuclear power works safely and reliably, the same cannot be said of renewable power generation on the scale being proposed.

Aside from the mind-boggling cost, WWS, as proposed by Jacobson and Delucchi, requires new, unproven technologies, rapidly falling manufacturing prices, and international cooperation unheard of today. Given the havoc caused by natural gas supply interruptions caused by Russia, would any sovereign nation trust a power grid that spans three continents and thousands of miles? A power grid that could be disrupted by terrorists or maniacal despots anywhere along its major arteries? Any way you look at renewable energy, it makes little sense.

Renewables Are an Unreasonable Deal

Perhaps the best way to look at running the world exclusively on renewable power is that it would cost $33,500 for every man, woman and child on Earth. People in developed nations might be willing to invest this much, but what of those living in under developed economies, where per capita yearly income can be less than $300? Nobody but deep green zealots would call this a reasonable deal. . . . The world's future energy needs can be met while reducing pollution and without bankrupting everyone on the planet—it just cannot be done using wind and solar energy.

EVALUATING THE AUTHOR'S ARGUMENTS:

Doug L. Hoffman argues that switching to an entirely renewable energy system is prohibitively expensive. Mark Z. Jacobson and Mark A. Delucchi, authors of the previous viewpoint, disagree. After reading both viewpoints, which set of authors do you think is right about whether the world can afford to switch to renewable energy? List in your answer at least two pieces of evidence that swayed you.

Cutting Carbon Emissions Will Slow Global Warming

Barry Brook

"Many credible studies show we can cost-effectively reduce greenhouse gas emissions, if the right policies are in place."

In the following viewpoint Barry Brook argues that carbon dioxide (CO_2) emissions from human activity are causing climate change. He explains that when oil, natural gas, and coal are burned for energy, the process deposits CO_2 into the atmosphere, along with other gases. Together these gases trap heat and prevent Earth from properly cooling itself. As a result, temperatures rise, which Brooks says will cause severe weather events, extinction, drought, and other catastrophic conditions. The best way to avert catastrophe, according to Brook, is to drastically cut the amount of CO_2 that gets put into the atmosphere. Curbing CO_2 emissions will require people to adopt non-carbon energy sources and significantly change their lifestyles, but Brook says it is worth it in order to avoid catastrophic climate change.

Brook is director of Climate Science at the Environment Institute at the University of Adelaide, Australia. He runs the website *BraveNewClimate,* where this viewpoint was originally published.

AS YOU READ, CONSIDER THE FOLLOWING QUESTIONS:
1. How many tons of carbon dioxide does Brook say humans have dumped into the atmosphere since the start of the Industrial Revolution?
2. How many parts per million does Brook say CO_2 concentrations rise per year?
3. By what percent does Brook say carbon emissions must be cut by the year 2050?

Earth's climate has always been dynamic and changeable. In the distant past there have been bouts of intense volcanic activity, periods when vast deserts spanned much of the globe, warm epochs when forests covered Antarctica, and glacial ages when much of Europe and North America were entombed under miles of ice. When large climatic changes occurred rapidly, a mass extinction of species was the result. Life later recovered, but this process inevitably took millions of years.

Just one species—humans—are now the agent of global change. As we develop our modern economies and settlements at a frantic rate, we have caused deforestation and fragmentation of natural habitats, over-hunting of wild species we use for food, chemical pollution of waterways and massive draw-downs of rivers, lakes and groundwater. These patently unsustainable human impacts are operating world-wide, are accelerating, and clearly constitute an environmental crisis. Yet the threat now posed by human-caused global warming is so severe that it may soon outpace all others.

Carbon Emissions Are the Source of the Problem

Recent global warming is caused principally by the release of long-buried fossil carbon, by burning oil, natural gas and coal. Since the furnaces of the industrial revolution were first ignited in the late 18th century, we have dumped more than a trillion tonnes of carbon dioxide (CO_2) into the atmosphere, as well as other heat-trapping greenhouse gases such as methane, nitrous oxide and ozone-destroying chlorofluorocarbons. The airborne concentration of CO_2 is now 38 per cent higher than at any time over the past million years (and perhaps much longer—information beyond this time is too sketchy to be sure). Average global temperature has risen about 0.8°C in the last two centuries, with almost two-thirds of that warming having occurred in just the last 50 years.

Complex computer simulation models of the atmosphere have been developed and refined for over 40 years. They are now sufficiently advanced that they can reproduce most of the major features of climate change observed over the last 150 years. Under a business-as-usual scenario, which assume a continued reliance on fossil fuels as our primary energy source, these models predict 1.8°C to 6.4°C of further global warming during the 21st century. There is also a real danger that we have reached or will soon reach tipping points that will cascade uncontrollably and take the future out of our hands. But much of the uncertainty represented in this wide range of possibilities relates to our inability to forecast the probable economic and technological development pathway global societies will take over the next few decades.

Year by year, our scientific understanding of climate science and responses of the Earth system continues to grow and mature.

> **FAST FACT**
>
> According to a 2009 study by National Oceanic and Atmospheric Administration senior scientist Susan Solomon, allowing atmospheric CO_2 to reach a peak level of 450–600 parts per million before CO_2 emissions are cut will be too late, because drastic increases in global temperature, rainfall, and sea level will be irreversible for more than one thousand years even if CO_2 emissions are completely stopped.

We Must Cut Our Carbon Emissions

In short, it remains within our power to anticipate many of the impacts of future global warming, and to make the key economic and

Americans Think the Government Should Regulate Greenhouse Gas Emissions

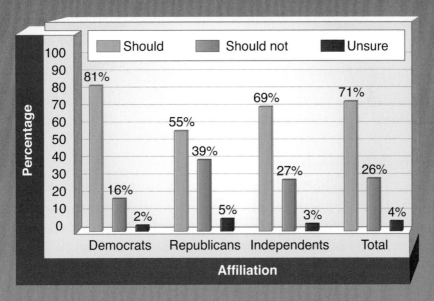

Question: "Do you think the federal government should or should not regulate the release of greenhouse gases from sources like power plants, cars, and factories in an effort to reduce global warming?"

Taken from: ABC News/*Washington Post* Poll. June 3–6, 2010.

technological choices required to substantially mitigate our carbon emissions. But will we act in time, and will it be with sufficient effort to avoid dangerous climate change?

Should we choose to take no effective action, we can expect increasingly severe consequences. For instance, beyond about 2°C of further warming, the Great Barrier Reef will be devastated. Extreme events will become much more frequent, such as storm surges adding to rising sea levels of many metres, threatening coastal cities. There is the possibility that a semi-persistent or more intense El Niño[1] will set in, leading to frequent failures of tropical monsoonal rains which

1. A weather pattern in which ocean warming and storms intensify.

provides the water required to feed billions of people. Above 3°C, up to half of all species may be consigned to extinction because of their inability to cope with such rapid and extreme changes.

Worryingly, even if we can manage to stabilise CO_2 concentrations at 450 parts per million (it is currently 387, and rising at 3 parts per million per year), we would still only have a roughly 50:50 chance of averting dangerous climate change. This will require a global cut in emissions of 50–85% by 2050 and certainly more than 90% for developed nations like Australia. Peak oil, global warming and long-term sustainability all require that we move rapidly to adopt sustainable, non-carbon energy sources, such as nuclear power and renewables (with the choice dictated largely by economic viability). Many credible studies show we can cost-effectively reduce greenhouse gas emissions. *If* the right policies are in place.

A Bleak Endowment

Unfortunately, there is little evidence so far that we, as individual countries or as a global collective of humanity, are taking meaningful action. Indeed, 'carbon intensity' (expressed as gross domestic product per tonne of carbon emitted) in developed nations such as the United States and Australia has actually increased over the last decade (2000–2010), the global rate of emissions growth risen from 1% to 3% per year, and total carbon emissions from all sources now exceed 9 billion tonnes a year. China overtook the United States in 2006 as the single biggest greenhouse polluter and will be producing twice as much CO_2 within little more than another decade at its present rate of economic activity.

This exponential growth in carbon-based energy, if sustained, will mean that over just the next 25 years, humans will emit into the atmosphere a volume of carbon that exceeds the total amount emitted during the 250-year industrial period of 1750 to 2000. Of particular concern is that long-lived greenhouse gases, such as CO_2, will continue to amplify global warming for centuries to come. For every five tonnes added during a year in which we dither about reducing emissions, one tonne will still be trapping heat in 1,000 years.

It is a bleak endowment to future generations.

Viewpoint

6

Cutting Carbon Emissions Will Hurt the Economy

"Are we really in a position right now to impose a huge added cost on society, burden our economic recovery, drive more manufacturing jobs overseas, . . . all for something that is inconsequential to the planet's climate?"

Alan Bressler

In the following viewpoint Alan Bressler argues that cutting carbon dioxide (CO_2) emissions is a very costly endeavor that will not necessarily benefit the planet. He argues it will cost billions of dollars and thousands of jobs in an effort to restrict companies and force them to reduce their CO_2 emissions. Worse, says Bressler, there is no proof that this strategy will have any effect on the planet's temperature: He says it is still unclear whether CO_2 emissions have anything to do with increasing temperatures. Bressler suggests that plans to reduce CO_2 emissions are more about expanding the government's size and power than saving the economy or the planet. He concludes that programs that seek to cut carbon emissions are bad for the economy and bad for America.

Bressler is a policy adviser to the Heartland Institute, an organization that promotes free-market solutions to public policy issues such as global warming.

AS YOU READ, CONSIDER THE FOLLOWING QUESTIONS:
1. How much does Bressler say it would cost the United States to control CO_2 emissions per year?
2. How many degrees Celsius would the global temperature be reduced if the Kyoto Protocol were strictly in place, according to Bressler?
3. What did a study from Spain's Juan Carlos University find about the effect the creation of green jobs has on other jobs?

Whe he initially laid out his CO_2 [carbon dioxide] cap-and-trade policy,[1] the president [Barack Obama] stated publicly his expectation that it would raise "revenue" (read: tax) of approximately $650 billion over eight years. . . .

All credible analyses of the costs of a cap-and-trade approach to controlling CO_2 emissions suggest it will cost the world 1 to 4 percent of global GDP [gross domestic product]. The United States is an approximately $14 trillion annual GDP economy. So for America, 1 percent = $140 billion annually, 2 percent = $280 billion annually, 3 percent = $420 billion annually, and 4 percent = $560 billion annually.

It Is Not Clear That Cutting Carbon Emissions Will Benefit the Planet

If all Annex I [industrialized countries and economies in transition] and II [developed countries that pay for costs of developing countries] nations had signed the Kyoto Protocol,[2] implemented it, met their CO_2 emissions reduction targets, and extended these protections in perpetuity, the most likely difference this would make to planetary temperatures by the year 2100 vs. business as usual would be approximately .13 to .20 degrees Celsius. In case you missed the decimal, that's less than a quarter of a degree Celsius, 91 years from

1. Cap-and-trade is a system in which companies or industries can "offset" restrictions by paying third parties that do not face the same restrictions to reduce their emissions instead. For example, a coal-fired power plant may offset excess emissions by preserving a tropical forest and/or paying another low-emitting company to share some of its unused carbon emission credits.
2. The Kyoto Protocol is an environmental treaty designed to curb global warming by reducing carbon dioxide emissions around the globe.

now, at a cost of 1 to 4 percent of global GDP. And that means 1 to 4 percent of global GDP not once but annually, from now until the Earth explodes from "global warming" or humanity comes to its senses. . . .

If it were clear that taking such drastic measures would surely avert a planetary crisis, there might be an argument for spending such enormous amounts, because the cost/benefit tradeoff would be obvious. But alas, computer models are not clear evidence of harm from anthropogenic CO_2 (they are merely predictions) and no such hard evidence exists. In fact, much evidence to the contrary has been known to scientists for many years, and more arrives almost daily.

At less than a quarter of a degree Celsius by the year 2100—an amount which cannot even be differentiated from natural climate variability—taking such measures today "for future generations" makes no sense at all. In fact, ironically enough, it fits precisely the term [former vice president and environmentalist] Al Gore has used to brand those who disagree with him: "morally reprehensible."

A Huge Drag on the Economy

It is thus clear that the Obama administration's cap-and-trade policy will be (a) environmentally inconsequential and (b) extremely costly. The administration also claims that cap-and-trade is a key to our economic growth and emergence from the current deep recession. But in addition to the direct cost (expressed above as a percentage of annual GDP), there is a substantial indirect cost to the economy that is conveniently overlooked by many proponents of cap-and-trade policy.

No one on the environmental left suggests with a straight face that cap-and-trade won't raise energy prices; actually, most proponents are rather proud of this fact and say "that's exactly the point." Raising energy prices has a demonstrable negative effect on economic growth. This is not just a computer model projection or hypothesis; it has been proven true in the real world over and over again. Witness the drag on the U.S. economy caused by high energy prices in the past, including as recently as the summer of 2008. Since it is a foregone conclusion that cap-and-trade will raise energy prices, it is safe to bet the farm that such a policy will have a long-term negative effect on U.S. GDP growth, in addition to the direct cost in the range of hundreds of billions of dollars per year.

President Barack Obama is among the supporters of cap-and-trade, which would provide economic incentives to limit pollution.

Annual U.S. GDP growth in the twentieth century averaged approximately 3 percent in real dollars. If we hinder this growth by even 1 percent of total GDP (one-third of our average GDP growth) through a cap-and-trade CO_2 policy, as many credible analyses show, it is difficult to see how such a policy can be viewed as creating future economic growth and a way out of the current recession.

Cutting Carbon Emissions Will Cost Jobs

Obama and left-leaning environmentalists also portray cap-and-trade as a means of creating "green" jobs. However, academic analyses of the potential green jobs created by the administration's cap-and-trade proposal, the green jobs elements of the recently passed stimulus bill, potential green jobs related to Obama's renewable energy standard preferences (25 percent of electricity from renewables by 2025), and the experiences with green job creation in many European Union countries all suggest that using such means to create job growth is a net negative to society.

A recently released study from Spain's Juan Carlos University on Spain's renewable energy initiatives, for example, found that for every "green" job that was created, 2.2 "dirty" jobs were destroyed. Yet Obama regularly holds Spain out as a shining example of the "green jobs" policy he favors.

Punishing fossil fuel–based energy, closing coal-fired power plants, shifting to alternative forms of energy with much higher costs, and transforming 100 years of energy use patterns overnight with the stroke of a pen will eliminate many jobs in the power and utility, heavy manufacturing, steel, cement, and other energy-intensive industries. Many of these jobs will simply head to countries without strict CO_2 emissions regulation. . . .

Cutting Carbon Emissions Will Grow the Government

Since cap and trade won't fix "global warming," will be very costly for a minuscule (if any) climatic benefit, won't be a net job creator for the U.S., and is a poor means of funding alternative energy R&D [research and development], might there be something else going on here? The answer lies in the numbers.

If 23 percent of the tax money raised from Obama's cap-and-trade policy is going toward alternative energy R&D, then 77 percent is

Americans Fear That Policies to Curb Global Warming Will Hurt the Economy

As Americans struggled with a recession, growing deficit, and an ongoing job slump, the majority feared that global warming reduction laws—such as those that seek to curb carbon dioxide emissions—will either definitely or probably hurt the economy.

Participants were asked whether they believed that the economy would be definitely hurt, unaffected, helped, or definitely helped by the new laws for the environment and for energy that are intended to combat global warming.

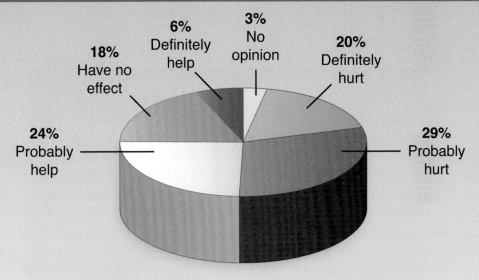

6% Definitely help

3% No opinion

18% Have no effect

20% Definitely hurt

24% Probably help

29% Probably hurt

Taken from: Gallup Poll, March 4–7, 2010.

going somewhere else. Where is all that money going? Most of it is going to two specific purposes.

First, a significant portion of this 77 percent will come right off the top and be used to fund the new gargantuan bureaucracy to administer CO_2 emissions regulations and the cap-and-trade program itself. During the debate over Lieberman-Warner-Boxer last summer,[3] it became obvious that 40 or more new agencies, departments, or other

3. Debated in June 2008, this bill would create a national cap-and-trade system for greenhouse gas emissions.

edifices of government would have to be created to administer the program. CO_2 emissions allowances have to be calculated, tracked, and enforced. The legislation would create an entirely new government commodities market in CO_2 emissions allowances out of thin air, and that would require regulation, monitoring, and other administrative efforts. These examples merely scratch the surface. . . .

A Strain on America

Are we really in a position right now to impose a huge added cost on society, burden our economic recovery, drive more manufacturing jobs overseas, and pay for tax breaks for people who don't pay taxes, all for something that is inconsequential to the planet's climate?

America may need a lifeline, but what it doesn't need is to be sold a lifeline that turns out to be a noose.

EVALUATING THE AUTHOR'S ARGUMENTS:

Alan Bressler argues that cutting carbon emissions will cost too much money. To what extent do you think money should be considered when talking about solutions to global warming? Should money be a primary consideration? Should it be low on the list of issues to consider? Explain how important you think the issue of cost is when considering solutions to global warming, and how you came to your opinion.

Facts About Global Warming

Editor's note: These facts can be used in reports or papers to reinforce or add credibility when making important points or claims.

Facts About Greenhouse Gases

A greenhouse gas (GHG) is any gaseous chemical compound that can absorb and emit infrared radiation—in other words, that can trap heat—in the earth's atmosphere.

The main GHGs are:
- water vapor
- carbon dioxide (CO_2)
- methane (CH_4)
- nitrous oxide (N_2O)
- ozone (O_3)
- compounds called halocarbons (fluorine, chlorine, and bromine).

According to the National Oceanic and Atmospheric Administration's Global Monitoring Division:
- Atmospheric CO_2 levels rose gradually from about 185 parts per million (ppm) in the last Ice Ages to about 278 ppm in the late 1700s, the eve of the Industrial Revolution.
- CO_2 levels have since risen to 290 ppm in 1900, 316 ppm in 1959, and 390 ppm in 2011.
- CO_2 levels have risen more in the past 220 years than in the previous 21,000 years.

No one knows exactly how much atmospheric carbon dioxide will guarantee a climate disaster. Instead, scientists use the term DAI, meaning the amount of CO_2 that represents Dangerous Anthropogenic (i.e., human-caused) Interference.

James Hansen of the NASA Goddard Institute for Space Studies estimates DAI to be at most 350 ppm.

According to the Natural Resources Defense Council (NRDC):

- The United States is the second-largest emitter (next to China) of greenhouse gases, accounting for 16 percent of the world's emissions, or 23.1 metric tons of CO_2 per American per year.
- China accounts for 17 percent of global emissions but, due to its much larger population, only 5.5 metric tons of CO_2 per person per year.

Facts About Global Temperatures

Global land-surface and oceanic temperature records are based on measurements collected by satellite observation, several thousand weather stations on land and on ships, and Antarctic research facilities.

Analysis of these data is performed at four main centers:

- University of East Anglia's Climatic Research Unit (UK)
- Met Office Hadley Center for Climate Prediction and Research (UK)
- NASA Goddard Institute for Space Studies (US)
- National Climatic Data Center (US)

According to the National Oceanic and Atmospheric Administration:

- Between 1906 and 2005, the earth's average surface temperature rose 0.74°C (1.33°F).
- 2001–2010 were ten of the warmest eleven years on record (since continuous global record keeping began in 1850).
- The years 2010 and 2005 are tied as the warmest years on record, with average temperatures 0.62°C (1.12°F) higher than the twentieth-century average.

According to the Intergovernmental Panel on Climate Change (IPCC):

- Global temperatures will rise on average between 1.1–6.4°C (2.0–11.5°F) by 2100.
- According the IPCC's *Fourth Assessment Report*, this rise is primarily the result of human activity:
    1) burning oil, coal, and natural gas to generate electricity for transportation and to operate businesses and homes;

2) burning of forests; and

3) converting forests to rangeland, agriculture, and cities.

Facts About Global Warming's Effect on Ecosystems and Species

According to the Intergovernmental Panel on Climate Change (IPCC):

- Increases in sea surface temperature of 1–3°C (1.8–5.4°F) would likely lead to widespread destruction of the world's coral reefs.
- If the global average temperature rise is more than 3.5°C (6.3°F), the IPCC predicts global species extinction rates of 40–70 percent.
- Some of the impacts of climate change likely to push endangered species closer to extinction are shrinking of glaciers and Arctic and Antarctic sea ice, with likely disappearance of summer sea ice in the Arctic by 2050; increased drought and desertification; and coastal flooding and erosion.

The Pew Center on Global Climate Change reports that since 1979, more than 20 percent of the polar ice cap has melted in response to increased surface air and ocean temperatures.

Facts About Global Warming Legislation

In 2009 the House of Representatives passed the American Clean Energy and Security Act (also known as the Waxman-Markey bill). It was the first bill passed by any house of Congress designed to curb global warming by reducing greenhouse gas emissions. Key provisions included:

1. Requiring electric utilities to meet 20 percent of electricity demand through renewable energy sources by 2050;
2. Allocating $190 billion in new federal subsidies for clean energy technology, electric car development, carbon capture and storage, and scientific research to counter global warming;
3. Reducing US greenhouse gas emissions by 83 percent of 2005 levels by 2050 through a cap-and-trade system similar to that in use in Europe. Cap-and-trade limits total CO_2 emissions and rewards better-performing producers with tradeable credits.

The Waxman-Markey bill died in the Senate in 2010. In the absence of congressional action on climate change, the Environmental Protection Agency took action in 2011 to declare CO_2 a pollutant, thereby allowing the regulation of CO_2 emissions from power plants and oil refineries under the Clean Air Act.

American Opinions About Global Warming

According to a February 2011 *Public Opinion Quarterly* survey, political disagreement over global warming depends partly on the language used to describe the issue:

- When asked if "global warming" is a real phenomenon, only 44.0 percent of Republicans said yes; however, when asked if "climate change" is real, 60.2 percent of Republicans said yes.
- Polled Democrats did not make that distinction: 86.9 percent said "global warming" was real, and 86.4 percent said "climate change" was real.

According to a 2010 poll by *USA Today* and the Gallup Organization:

- 56 percent of Americans favor Congress passing legislation that would regulate energy output from private companies in an attempt to reduce global warming;
- 40 percent oppose such legislation;
- 4 percent are unsure.

A 2010 ABC News/*Washington Post* poll found:

- 71 percent of Americans think the government should regulate the release of greenhouse gases from sources such as power plants, cars, and factories in an effort to reduce global warming;
- 26 percent think the government should not do this;
- 4 percent are unsure.

A 2010 Virginia Commonwealth University Life Sciences Survey revealed the following opinions and attitudes about global warming:

- 54 percent of Americans think global warming is a major problem;
- 23 percent think it is a minor problem;
- 19 percent think it is not a problem at all;
- 5 percent are unsure;

- 48 percent think global warming is a proven fact and is mostly caused by emissions from cars and industrial facilities such as power plants and factories;
- 16 percent think global warming is a proven fact caused mostly by natural changes that have nothing to do with emissions from cars and industrial facilities;
- 29 percent think global warming is a theory that has not yet been proven;
- 7 percent are unsure;
- 22 percent think government regulations to reduce global warming will help a lot;
- 39 percent think government regulations to reduce global warming will help some;
- 15 percent think government regulations to reduce global warming will not help much;
- 19 percent think government regulations to reduce global warming will not help at all;
- 4 percent are unsure.

A 2010 poll conducted jointly by CBS News and the *New York Times* found:
- 38 percent of Americans think global warming is an environmental problem that is causing a serious impact now;
- 29 percent think the impact of global warming will not happen until sometime in the future;
- 24 percent think global warming will not have a serious impact at all;
- 5 percent think global warming does not exist;
- 4 percent are unsure.

Organizations to Contact

The editors have compiled the following list of organizations concerned with the issues debated in this book. The descriptions are derived from materials provided by the organizations. All have publications or information available for interested readers. The list was compiled on the date of publication of the present volume; the information provided here may change. Be aware that many organizations take several weeks or longer to respond to inquiries, so allow as much time as possible for the receipt of requested materials.

American Coalition for Clean Coal Electricity (ACCCE)
333 John Carlyle St., Ste. 530
Alexandria, VA 22314
(703) 684-6292
e-mail: info@cleancoalusa.org
website: http://cleancoalusa.org

A front group and public relations arm of the coal industry founded in 2008, the coalition encourages the production of electricity from coal (which it promotes as a "clean," abundant, and affordable fuel). The ACCCE opposes Environmental Protection Agency regulation of greenhouse gases. Instead, it supports investment in advanced technologies to capture and store CO_2 emissions from the burning of fossil fuels. Available on the website are numerous policy papers and videos, information on zero-emission coal plants, and statistics comparing coal with other energy sources.

Center for the Study of Carbon Dioxide and Global Change
PO Box 25697
Tempe, AZ 85285-5697
(480) 966-3719
website: www.co2science.org

The nonprofit center is a project of three prominent global warming skeptics: geographer Craig D. Idso, botanist Keith E. Idso, and their physicist father, Sherwood B. Idso. Available on the website are numerous position papers, the weekly online newsletter *CO₂ Science*, and experiments/studies purporting to show that CO_2 benefits plants and plays no role in ocean acidification or atmospheric warming.

Environmental Protection Agency (EPA), Climate Change Site

Ariel Rios Bldg., 1200 Pennsylvania Ave. NW
Washington, DC 20460
(202) 272-0167
website: www.epa.gov

The EPA is the federal agency in charge of protecting the environment and controlling pollution, mainly by issuing and enforcing regulations such as air quality and emissions standards, identifying and fining polluters, and cleaning up polluted sites. The agency's climate change site is a source of climate-change indicators, scientific studies, explanations of federal greenhouse gas policy and regulatory initiatives, and FAQs for students and citizens.

George C. Marshall Institute

1625 K St. NW, Ste. 1050
Washington, DC 20006
(202) 296-9655
fax: (202) 296-9714
e-mail: info@marshall.org
website: www.marshall.org

The institute, a nonprofit organization founded in 1984, takes a minority position on global warming science. It argues that the scientific view of the causes and effects of global climate change, including the contribution of human activity and the danger to animal and plant species, is unproven and flawed. The institute publishes reports opposing restrictions on greenhouse gas emissions such as *Considering Climate and Energy Policy in 2011*, physics professor William Happer's 2009 congressional testimony about the benefits of increased carbon dioxide in the atmosphere, and regular *George C. Marshall Institute Studies*. The institute's publications include the book *Shattered Consensus: The True State of Global Warming* and many studies, including "Natural Climate Variability" and "Climate Issues and Questions."

Global Warming International Center (GWIC)
PO Box 50303
Palo Alto, CA 94303
(630) 910-1551
fax: (630) 910-1561
website: www.globalwarming.net

GWIC is an international body that disseminates information on science and policy concerning global warming. It serves both governmental and nongovernmental organizations as well as industries in more than one hundred countries. The center sponsors unbiased research supporting the understanding of global warming, as well as projects such as Himalayan reforestation and tracking of the short-term and long-term economic costs of global warming on specific localities around the world.

Greenpeace USA
702 H St. NW, Ste. 300
Washington, DC 20001
(202) 462-1177
website: www.greenpeace.org

Greenpeace has long campaigned against environmental degradation, urging government and industry to curb climate change, protect forests, and stop destruction of marine ecosystems and species. Its activism is based on direct confrontation and interference with its opponents' activities as well as exposing harmful practices. Greenpeace publishes reports and pamphlets about climate and energy, forests, and genetic engineering of crops.

Heartland Institute
19 South LaSalle St., Ste. 903
Chicago, IL 60603
(312) 377-4000
website: www.heartland.org

The institute is a nonprofit libertarian research and education organization. A vigorous opponent of government regulation of greenhouse gas emissions, it challenges the scientific consensus on global warming and sponsors and publishes research by global warming skeptics. Publications include books, videos, and a monthly newsletter.

International Panel on Climate Change (IPCC)
IPCC Secretariat, c/o World Meteorological Organization
7 bis Avenue de la Paix, C.P. 2300
CH-1211 Geneva 2, Switzerland
(+41) 22-730-8208
fax: (+41) 22-730-8205
e-mail: IPCC-Sec@wmo.int
website: www.ipcc.ch

The IPCC, created by the World Meteorological Organization (WMO) and the United Nations Environment Programme (UNEP) in 1988, evaluates global climate change and the role of human activity in global warming, based on accumulated international scientific evidence and peer-reviewed published findings. The *IPCC Fourth Assessment Report* (known as AR4), issued in 2007 and available in summary and full forms on the website, is an urgent call to action. It concludes that global warming is undeniable; that it is due to greenhouse gas emissions caused by human activity; that atmospheric concentrations of carbon dioxide, nitrous oxide, and methane are far higher than they have been for 650,000 years; and that a "business as usual" response will lead to catastrophic species extinction. In addition to the AR4, the IPCC publishes research papers on sea level rise; updates on the *IPCC Fifth Assessment Report* (AR5), due in 2014; and a wide range of press releases, speeches, and graphs.

Met Office Hadley Centre
Met Office, FitzRoy Rd.
Exeter, Devon EX1 3PB, United Kingdom
e-mail: enquiries@metoffice.gov.uk
website: www.metoffice.gov.uk

The center is the United Kingdom's official agency for climate change research, focusing particularly on scientific issues. This agency advises the British government on the latest developments in climate change science and recommends policies to mitigate global warming's likely adverse impacts.

National Corporation for Atmospheric Research (NCAR)
PO Box 3000
Boulder, CO 80307-3000

(303) 497-1000
website: www2.ncar.edu

In cooperation with university research departments, the federally funded NCAR plans and conducts atmospheric experiments to better understand the physical and biological processes of climate change, from laboratories in Colorado and a solar observatory in Hawaii. Study results, a directory of research topics, and numerous school and community projects are available on the website.

National Renewable Energy Laboratory (NREL)
1617 Cole Blvd.
Golden, CO 80401-3393
(303) 275-3000
website: www.nrel.gov

The National Renewable Energy Laboratory is the US Department of Energy's laboratory for renewable energy research, development, and deployment, and a leading laboratory for energy efficiency. The laboratory's mission is to develop renewable energy and energy-efficient technologies and practices, advance related science and engineering, and transfer knowledge and innovations to address the nation's energy and environmental goals.

Pacific Institute, Global Change Program
654 13th St., Preservation Park
Oakland, CA 94612
(510) 251-1600
fax: (510) 251-2203
e-mail: info@pacinst.org
website: www.pacinst.org

The institute's programs focus on developing sustainable practices that combine economic development and environmental protection in a warming world. Managing and protecting global water supplies is a main priority. Publications include the series *The World's Water*, research reports, case studies, and legislative opinion papers.

Pembina Institute for Appropriate Development
PO Box 7558
Drayton Valley, AB, T7A 1S7 Canada

(780) 542-6272
fax: (780) 542-6464
website: www.pembina.org

The institute is an independent, nonprofit environmental policy research and education organization. Its major policy research and education programs are in the areas of sustainable energy, climate change, environmental governance, ecological fiscal reform, sustainability indicators, and the environmental impacts of the energy industry. The institute pioneers practical solutions to issues affecting human health and the environment across Canada. Numerous papers and reports relating to climate change issues are available on the institute's website.

Pew Center on Global Climate Change
2101 Wilson Blvd., Ste. 550
Arlington, VA 22201
(703) 516-4146
fax: (703) 841-1422
website: www.pewclimate.org

The center is an independent nonprofit research organization. Initiatives include the Make an Impact program, which shows individuals how to reduce their carbon footprint; congressional testimony; publication of the latest peer-reviewed scientific studies on global warming (as well as clear primers for laymen such as "Climate Change 101"); and partnerships between businesses and nongovernmental organizations to come up with innovative ideas for addressing climate change. The website is a comprehensive resource for student researchers.

Renewable Energy Policy Project (REPP)
1612 K St. NW, Ste. 202
Washington, DC 20006
(202) 293-2898
fax: (202) 298-5857
e-mail: info2@repp.org
website: www.repp.org

The Renewable Energy Policy Project provides useful information about solar, hydrogen, biomass, wind, hydrogen, and other forms of renewable energy.

Sierra Club
85 Second St.
San Francisco, CA 94105
(415) 977-5500
fax: (415) 977-5799
e-mail: info@sierraclub.org
website: www.sierraclub.org

The Sierra Club is a grassroots organization that promotes the protection and conservation of natural resources. It publishes the bimonthly magazine *Sierra*, the monthly Sierra Club activist resource *The Planet*, and numerous books and pamphlets.

Union of Concerned Scientists (UCS)
2 Brattle Sq.
Cambridge, MA 02238-9105
(617) 547-5552
website: www.ucsusa.org

UCS works to advance responsible public policy in areas where science and technology play a vital role. Its programs focus on safe and renewable energy technologies, transportation reform, arms control, and sustainable agriculture. UCS publications include the quarterly magazine *Nucleus*, the briefing papers *Motor-Vehicle Fuel Efficiency and Global Warming* and *Global Environmental Problems: A Status Report*, and the book *Cool Energy: The Renewable Solution to Global Warming*.

US Global Change Research Program (GCRP)
1717 Pennsylvania Ave. NW, Ste. 250
Washington, DC 20006
(202) 223-6262
fax: (202) 223-3065
website: www.globalchange.gov

Mandated by Congress in 1990, the GCRP conducts the National Climate Assessment, a comprehensive status report on the extent and impacts of global warming across the United States. The assessment includes comparisions of actual observations with predictions of computer models. The website offers interactive maps and tools that give clear climate information broken down by US region, an image gallery, and an archive of assessment summaries.

Books

Hannah, Lee, ed. *Saving a Million Species: Extinction Risk from Climate Change*. Washington, DC: Island, 2011. A collection of expert opinions on the extent of extinctions resulting from global warming and conservation strategies to prevent biodiversity loss.

Hansen, James. *Storms of My Grandchildren: The Truth About the Coming Climate Catastrophe and Our Last Chance to Save Humanity*. New York: Bloomsbury USA, 2009. Hansen, director of NASA's Goddard Institute for Space Studies, argues that global warming is a serious threat to the habitability of the planet. Hansen's vision is dark but not hopeless: His policy recommendations to avoid a runaway greenhouse effect, which he calls the Venus syndrome, include a halt to coal burning and the building of advanced nuclear power plants.

Hertsgaard, Mark. *Hot: Living Through the Next Fifty Years on Earth*. New York: Houghton Mifflin Harcourt, 2011. An optimistic survey of techniques for "avoiding the unmanageable and managing the unavoidable" effects of global warming, including innovative flood plans in the Netherlands, floating agriculture in Bangladesh, and simple precautions such as painting flat roofs white to reflect more heat.

Hulme, Mike. *Why We Disagree About Climate Change: Understanding Controversy, Inaction, and Opportunity*. Cambridge, UK: Cambridge University Press, 2009. British climatologist Hulme compares scientific, economic, political, psychological, and religious views of climate change in an attempt to explain why the issue is so controversial, despite convincing evidence that global warming science is not a hoax and that global warming poses serious risks to humankind.

Lappé, Anna. *Diet for a Hot Planet: The Climate Crisis at the End of Your Fork and What You Can Do About It*. New York: Bloomsbury USA, 2010. Arguing that industrial agriculture is a major contributor to greenhouse gases, the author presents a "climate-friendly diet" based on eating more plants and unprocessed foods from local, organic producers.

Oreskes, Naomi, and Erik M. Conway. *Merchants of Doubt: How a Handful of Scientists Obscured the Truth on Issues from Tobacco Smoke to Global Warming*. New York: Bloomsbury USA, 2011. The authors argue that global warming skeptics are misusing science for political and commercial ends. Tactics such as casting doubt on settled science and accusing researchers of fraud succeed because the more these charges are repeated in the media, the more they acquire an air of legitimacy, confusing and misleading the public into delaying meaningful action to eliminate fossil fuel use.

Singer, S. Fred, Craig Idso, and Robert M. Carter. *Climate Change Reconsidered: 2011 Interim Report of the Nongovernmental International Panel on Climate Change*. Chicago: Heartland Institute, 2011. Published by an anti-government-regulation think tank and written by well-known global warming skeptics, this book should not be confused with the UN Intergovernmental Panel on Climate Change (IPCC) Assessment Reports. The authors claim that IPCC forecasts are unscientific and biased, that there is no evidence that human activity is affecting global temperatures, and that the planet needs more, not less, atmospheric carbon dioxide. The report concludes that a warmer world will increase biodiversity and plant yields, improve human health, and decrease extreme weather.

Periodicals and Internet Sources

Begley, Sharon. "Are You Ready for More?," *Newsweek*, May 29, 2011.

Biello, David. "Can Geoengineering Save the World from Global Warming?," *Scientific American*, February 25, 2011.

Board on Atmospheric Sciences and Climate, National Research Council. *America's Climate Choices*, Washington, DC: National Academies Press, May 2011. www.nap.edu/catalog.php?record_id=12781.

Cook, John. "Empirical Evidence That Humans Are Causing Global Warming," Skeptical Science, June 26, 2010. www.skepticalscience.com/empirical-evidence-for-global-warming.htm.

Economist. "One Degree Over," March 17, 2011.

Epstein, Paul. "An Era of Tornadoes: How Global Warming Causes Wild Winds," Atlantic Monthly, July 8, 2011.

Friedman, Thomas L. "Global Weirding Is Here," New York Times, February 17, 2010.

Gillis, Justin. "In Weather Chaos, a Case for Global Warming," New York Times, August 14, 2010.

———. "A Message from Mother Nature?," New York Times Upfront, vol. 143, September 20, 2010. http://teacher.scholastic.com/scholasticnews/indepth/upfront/features/index.asp?article=f092010_global.

Houston Chronicle. "The Heat Is On: New Data Debunk Claims That Global Warming Is Hype," January 26, 2009. www.chron.com/opinion/editorials/article/The-heat-is-on-New-data-debunk-claims-that-1728318.php.

Kamp, Jurriaan. "There Is Plenty Renewable Energy to Fight Global Warming," Huffington Post, December 30, 2009. www.huffingtonpost.com/jurriaan-kamp/there-is-plenty-renewable_b_397237.html.

Koch, Wendy. "U.S. Cities Prepare to Adapt to Climate Change," USA Today, August 15, 2011.

Kolbert, Elizabeth. "Hurricane Irene and Global Warming: A Glimpse of the Future?," New Yorker, August 28, 2011.

Lachman, Steve. "Global Warming Can't Wait," Centre Daily Times (State College, PA), February 8, 2011. www.centredaily.com/2011/02/08/2504838/global-warming-cant-wait.html.

Lemonick, Michael D. "Even Plants May Not Like a Warmer World," Time Science, January 15, 2010. www.time.com/time/health/article/0,8599,1954190,00.html.

Mohan, Geoff. "Global Warming Effect Seen in Pole-to-Pole Data-Gathering Flights," Greenspace, Los Angeles Times, September 7, 2011. http://latimesblogs.latimes.com/greenspace/2011/09/global-warming-climate-change-seen-in-data-gathering.html.

National Wildlife Federation. "How Animals Fight Global Warming," January 6, 2010. www.nwf.org/News-and-Magazines/National-Wildlife/Animals/Archives/2010/How-Animals-Fight-Global-Warming.aspx.

Newell, Philip. "Five Plants You've Never Heard of That Can Slow Climate Change," *Nourishing the Planet,* Worldwatch Institute, August 9, 2011. http://blogs.worldwatch.org/nourishingtheplanet/five-plants-you%E2%80%99ve-never-heard-of-that-can-slow-climate-change.

Orcutt, Mike. "The Heat Was On: Atmospheric CO_2 Triggered a Global Warming Event 40 Million Years Ago," *Scientific American,* November 4, 2010.

Revkin, Andrew. "Can Clearer Language Clear Up Climate Change Disputes?," *Dot Earth, New York Times*, August 30, 2011. http://dotearth.blogs.nytimes.com/2011/08/30/can-clearer-language-clear-up-climate-disputes/?scp=3&sq=global%20warming&st=Search.

Robock, Alan. "20 Reasons Why Geoengineering May Be a Bad Idea," *Bulletin of the Atomic Scientists*, vol. 64, no. 2, May/June 2008.

Schiermeier, Quirin. "Biodiversity's Ills Not All Down to Climate Change," *Nature*, March 20, 2011. www.nature.com/news/2011/110320/full/news.2011.170.html.

Shafy, Samiha. "Can CO2 Catchers Combat Climate Change?," *Der Spiegel Online*, January 15, 2010. www.spiegel.de/international/world/0,1518,672072,00.html.

Swemson, F. "The Global Warming Hoax: How Soon We Forget," *American Thinker,* July 16, 2011. www.americanthinker.com/2011/07/the_global_warming_hoax_how_soon_we_forget.html.

Vergano, Dan. "Can Geoengineering Put the Freeze on Global Warming?," *USA Today*, February 25, 2011.

Walsh, Bryan. "Vanishing Act: How Climate Change Is Causing a New Age of Extinction," *Time*, Special Environment Issue, April 13, 2009.

Witze, Alexandra. "Swift Action to Cut Greenhouse Emissions Could Save Polar Bears," *Science News*, January 15, 2011.

Websites

Skeptical Science (www.skepticalscience.com). Dedicated to effectively debating and debunking climate change pseudoscience and denial, this site refutes, in simple language or in-depth discussion, more than 160 arguments made by global warming skeptics. Useful resources include dozens of climate-change charts and graphs, mobile device apps, and free downloads such as *The Scientific Guide to Global Warming Skepticism*.

Stop Global Warming (www.stopglobalwarming.org). This nonpartisan clearinghouse of global warming information includes an updated news archive, lists of recommended books and DVDs, and a Virtual March petition to lawmakers to demand a freeze and reduction of carbon dioxide emissions. Useful resources include a special section on classroom/student activities.

Union of Concerned Scientists, Global Warming 101 (www.ucsu sa.org/global_warming/global_warming_101). UCS is a US-based organization of professional scientists and interested nonprofessionals that lobby government and educate the public on science and technology issues. The website offers numerous articles on global warming science and solutions, as well as analyses of climate change effects broken down by US regions.

Index

Power grid
  cost of upgrading, 102
  need for investment in, 96

R
Rainfall, extreme, 64–65
Ramanathan, Veerabhadran, 74
Raplet, Chris, 14
Rare-earth metals, 91
Renewable energy
  switching to, can prevent
    global warming, 86–97
  switching to, if prohibitively
    expensive, 98–103
  total availability of, *95*
The Resilient Earth (blog), 99
Robock, Alan, 9
Royal Society of London, 7
Russia, increase in agricultural
  land in, 58

S
Schmitt, Harrison H., 21
Sea level
  global average, trend in, *17*
  rise in, 42, 45, 63–64
Snow cover, Northern
  Hemisphere, 26
  trend in, *17*
Solar panels, *102*
Solar power
  cost of electricity from, *vs.*
    other generation sources,
    101
  energy available from
    globally, 89
  footprint of, 91

reduction in CO_2 emissions
  per household, 93
Solar power plants
  cost of, 100–101
  numbers needed to produce
    84% of global energy needs
    in 2030, 99
Solomon, Susan, 106
Soot (black carbon), 76, 78,
  83
Soybeans, 54, 58
Stanford University, 87
Sulfur aerosols, 7–8, 84–85
Sunspot cycle, 15
Surveys
  on causes of global warming,
    28
  on government regulation of
    greenhouse gas emissions,
    107
  on impact of environmental/
    energy laws on economy,
    115
  on link between climate
    change and extreme
    weather events, 70
  on perceived threat of global
    warming, *47*

T
Taylor, James, 56
Temperature
  consequences of 6 degree rise,
    42
Trenberth, Kevin, 65
Twentieth Century Reanalysis
  Project, 69

Picture Credits

© AP Images, 41

© AP Images/Roberto Candia, 37

© AP Images/Christopher Patrick Grant, 48

© AP Images/NASA, 11

© AP Images/NOAA, 66

© Aurora Photos/Alamy, 26

© Juan Barreto/AFP/Getty Images, 77

© Matt Cardy/Getty Images, 102

© Corbis Flirt/Alamy, 84

Gale/Cengage Learning, 17, 28, 47, 54, 59, 95, 101, 107, 115

© Mike Kipling Photography/Alamy, 90

© Nagelestock.com/Alamy, 73

© NCAR/Photo Researchers, Inc., 35

© Janek Skarzynski/AFP/Getty Images, 113

© World History Archive/Alamy, 14